AS Law
UNIT 1

Module 1: Law Making

Rosemary

Series Editor:

Philip Allan Updates
Market Place
Deddington
Oxfordshire
OX15 0SE

Tel: 01869 338652
Fax: 01869 337590
e-mail: sales@philipallan.co.uk
www.philipallan.co.uk

© Philip Allan Updates 2003

ISBN 0 86003 936 6

This guide has been written specifically to support students preparing for the
AQA AS Law Unit 1 examination. The content has been neither approved nor
endorsed by AQA and remains the sole responsibility of the author.

Printed by Information Press, Eynsham, Oxford

Contents

Introduction

■ ■ ■

Content Guidance

■ ■ ■

Questions and Answers

Introduction

About this guide

This study guide is written for students following the AQA AS Law course. It deals with the Unit 1 specification **Law Making**. The topics in the module are designed to provide a sound introduction to how law is made in the English legal system. They examine the different ways in which laws arise and the involvement in these processes of the bodies of the European Union, the Houses of Parliament and judges. There are three sections to this guide:

- **Introduction** — this provides advice on how to use the guide, an explanation of the skills required to complete Unit 1 successfully and guidance on revision techniques.
- **Content Guidance** — this gives a broad overview of the law-making processes. The subject matter is broken down into manageable sections for study and learning. It contains references to cases which need to be studied more fully to achieve a sounder understanding.
- **Questions and Answers** — this provides examples of AS questions with, in most cases, both A-grade and C-grade answers. These are interspersed with examiner comments so that you can see how the marks are awarded.

How to use this guide

The Content Guidance section sets out the content for Unit 1, breaking it down into manageable sections for study and learning. It also contains references to cases which you will need to look at for a fuller understanding of each topic. It is not intended to be a comprehensive and detailed set of notes for this module — you will need to supplement this material with further reading from textbooks and case studies.

At the end of each section you will find it useful to compile a summary of the factual material under the appropriate headings. Additional material gained from wider reading and research should also be incorporated into the summary. You are advised to test yourself by using the sample questions given in the Question and Answer section. At the end of each topic you should study the question and write a full answer. On completing this, study the A-grade answer and compare it with your own. The examiner comments will help you to learn how you can use your knowledge and understanding most effectively to obtain higher marks.

Learning strategies

To be successful at AS, it is essential to build up a good set of notes. These notes need to be laid out clearly under the headings used in the Content Guidance section. Your notes should contain accurate definitions using the correct legal terminology, together with detailed explanations and relevant statutory and case references. One way to learn the relevant cases is to write the case names, key facts and the legal principles established in the various areas of law studied onto cards, which can be revised in free moments.

It is also important to undertake wider reading using a variety of sources — the law pages in newspapers, books and the internet — accompanied by sound note taking. Any notes from these sources should be included with your class notes. A good website to look at is that of the UK Parliament (**www.parliament.uk**), which allows access to the website for the European Union. Both contain very useful information on how laws come about.

Revision planning

You should have built up a file of notes while working through this unit. It is essential that you learn the basic factual information as you study each topic. This should not be left until the revision stage — otherwise there will be too much detailed knowledge to absorb. The topics learnt for one AS unit must not be confused with those learnt for another.

Plan your revision time carefully by setting a realistic timetable. One way to do this is to divide the topics to match your available revision sessions. Work for short sessions with planned breaks. Organise your work. The revision period is a time to go over your notes and reduce them to manageable proportions.

You may find it useful to:
- Rewrite your notes, focusing on the important areas which you need to remember.
- Condense the material to make it easier to learn. This is an active way of learning as it helps to focus on the main points.
- Ask a friend or family member to test you, to help with your learning process.
- Attempt some exam questions — practise writing them in the time limit.

Assessment objectives

Assessment objectives (AOs) are common to both AS and A2 units and are intended to assess candidates' ability to:
- recall, select, deploy and develop knowledge and understanding of legal principles accurately by means of example and citation
- analyse legal material, issues and situations, and evaluate and apply the appropriate legal rules and principles
- present a logical and coherent argument, communicating relevant material in a clear and effective manner, using appropriate legal terminology

The examination

In the Unit 1 examination there are five questions to choose from and you are required to answer *two* of them. All of the questions are in two parts and you do need to answer both parts. The examination is 1 hour long.

The first part of the question usually requires a clear description of the main facts of the topic. You will also find that in almost every question you will be required to illustrate your answer by using examples and/or case/statute references. It is very important to do this if it is required because, no matter how good the rest of the answer is, there is usually a maximum number of marks which can be awarded for answers with no illustration, so without them you can never get into the top mark band.

The second part of the question tends to require more analysis than simple explanation. Be careful, though, because sometimes the first part of the question requires the analysis. The second part of the question may also be on another area of law; for example, (a) could be on the parliamentary process and (b) on influences on Parliament. You should read both parts of the question; there is little point in answering part (a) if you find that you cannot answer part (b). By reading *all* the questions through first you can also avoid the problem of writing the answer to what seems to be an easy part (a) only to find too late that part (b) is much more difficult.

Another factor you should take into consideration when choosing the questions to answer is the way in which the marks are allocated. Each question is marked out of a total of 30 marks. This total can be split into two 15-mark parts, or either part (a) or part (b) can be 10 or 20 marks. It is important when deciding which questions to answer that you are aware of these mark allocations.

Planning is an important tool in achieving good marks in the exam. Time spent in making a few notes before you start writing is not wasted. Noting down a few key words/phrases and case/statute references helps to focus your mind on the answer. Make sure that you do not spend too long on one part of the question to the detriment of the other part. If you do have any time left over, read through your answer to see if you can add any extra, relevant material.

Content
Guidance

The material covered in Unit 1 is divided into six sections. They are all concerned with law-making processes. All sections need to be studied in some detail and the relationship between them recognised. They should be related to the areas of substantive law studied in Unit 3 both to support your evidence and to illustrate how the law works. The areas covered in this unit are:

European law
- Sources of European law
- How European law takes effect
- The European institutions
- The process of making European Union law
- The European Court of Justice
- The effect of EU membership on parliamentary supremacy

Statute law
- How statutes are created
- The doctrine of parliamentary supremacy

Delegated legislation
- Types of delegated legislation
- Control of delegated legislation
- The effectiveness of the controls on delegated legislation
- The necessity for delegated legislation
- Disadvantages of delegated legislation

Influences on Parliament
- Political pressures
- Law reform agencies
- Pressure groups
- Public opinion
- The media

Statutory interpretation
- Approaches to interpretation
- Presumptions
- Rules of language
- Aids to statutory interpretation

Judicial precedent
- The hierarchy of the courts
- Law reporting
- How judges avoid following precedent
- The advantages and disadvantages of judicial precedent

European law

Sources of European law

When the UK joined the European Community on 1 January 1973, a new source of law, European law, came into existence. European legislation consists of **treaties**, which are primary sources of law, and **regulations**, **directives** and **decisions**, which are all secondary sources of law. The power to make the last three is found under Article 249 of the Treaty of Rome, which created the European Economic Community in 1957.

Treaties

These primary sources of law are created by the member states, signed by the heads of government and, when ratified, automatically become part of the law in the member states. The European Communities Act 1972 s.2(1) implemented this in the UK. Treaties lay down the general aims of the European Union (EU) and also create some rights and obligations. If treaty provisions do not set out clear rights or duties, but are only statements of policy or intent, detailed legislation has to be enacted before they can be enforced.

Regulations

As soon as regulations come into force they automatically become law in the member states with no need for domestic legislation to be created to implement them. They are the closest thing to an Act of Parliament. Regulations cannot be amended or prevented from coming into force by a member state. The case of *Leonesio* v *Italian Agriculture Minister* (1973) established that if an existing national Act conflicts with a regulation, the regulation must be applied. In this case the Italian government had no power to block payments, despite the fact that the Italian Constitution required legislation to authorise government expenditure.

Directives

These are used to bring about harmonisation of the laws within the member states. As they set out broad objectives, they are not as precisely worded as regulations. Directives may be addressed to specific member states, requiring them to make changes in their law within a certain period of time, in order to bring them into line with the EU. Each state can decide the process by which it does this. In the UK, directives are usually implemented by statutory instrument. The Unfair Terms in Consumer Contract Regulations 1995 implemented the Unfair Contract Terms Directive 1994. Occasionally, as for the Consumer Protection Act 1987, an Act of Parliament may be used.

Decisions

These may be addressed to either a member state or an individual person or company. They are binding only on the recipient and require them to perform/refrain from an action, or confer rights or obligations on them.

How European law takes effect

All treaty articles, regulations and some decisions have **direct applicability**, because they take immediate effect as domestic law in the member states. In *Re Tachographs: EC Commission* v *UK* (1979) the European Court of Justice (ECJ) said that regulations automatically become law in the member states.

EU legislation can also have **direct effect**, which means that it creates individual rights which can be enforced through the national courts of the member states. This direct effect can be further divided into **vertical direct effect**, which gives individuals rights against the state, and **horizontal direct effect**, giving rights to individuals against other individuals and organisations.

The issue of direct effect was first considered in *Van Gend en Loos* (1963). If the treaty provisions are unconditional, clear and precise, and no further legislation is necessary to implement them, they have direct effect, both vertical and horizontal. In *Macarthys Ltd* v *Smith* (1980) Mrs Smith was entitled to the same rate of pay as her male predecessor under Article 141 of the Treaty of Rome — equal pay for men and women doing the same job.

Direct effect, both vertical and horizontal, also applies to regulations.

Directives are not directly applicable as they require some form of legislation to implement them. Their direct effect was established in *Van Duyn* v *Home Office* (1974). The Home Office had refused Van Duyn permission to enter the UK because of her membership of a religious group which the government wished to exclude. Van Duyn argued that this was contrary to the article in the Treaty of Rome granting freedom of movement. The UK government responded by saying that exceptions were allowed on policy grounds. A later directive said that public policy could only be invoked where public conduct was an issue and Van Duyn had done nothing that justified exclusion. When the case was referred to the ECJ, it found that a clear and unconditional obligation was conferred on the government and created enforceable rights.

An individual may bring an action even if the directive has not been implemented by the state or the implementation is defective. If the directive is clear and gives individual rights, it has vertical direct effect. As directives impose obligations on states, they do not have horizontal direct effect: *Duke* v *GEC Reliance Ltd* (1988).

However, the ECJ has defined the state very broadly. In *Marshall* v *Southampton and South West Hampshire Area Health Authority* (1986), Mrs Marshall's employers, the Health

Authority, were considered a public body and part of the state. She was able to rely on the Equal Treatment Directive.

The principle of **indirect effect** arises from *von Colson* v *Nordrhein–Westfalen* (1984). National courts must interpret national laws in the light of the wording and the purpose of the directive, whether it was implemented or not. This was confirmed in *Marleasing SA* v *La Comercial Internacional de Alimentacion SA* (1990).

The ECJ has made it possible for an individual to be compensated with a payment of damages from the member state which has failed to implement a directive within the time limit. This was introduced in *Italy* v *Francovich* (1992), where Francovich was unable to receive any wages due to him when the firm he worked for went bankrupt. The Italian government had failed to set up a scheme to provide for this situation, despite it being the subject of a directive. The ECJ said that Francovich had a right to damages from the Italian government.

In *Brasserie du Pêcheur SA* v *Federation of Republic of Germany* and *R* v *Secretary of State for Transport, ex parte Factortame Ltd (No 4)* (1996), the ECJ held that governments could be held liable for financial loss which resulted from their breach of EU law. Three conditions had to be met:
- the rule which was breached is intended to confer rights on the individuals
- the breach has to be sufficiently serious
- there must be a direct causal link between the breach and the damage

The European institutions

Under the Treaty of Rome 1957 four key institutions were created in order to carry out the functions of the European Community. These consist of:
- the Council of Ministers
- the Commission
- the European Parliament
- the European Court of Justice (see pp. 13–14)

The first three all have a role to play in the creation of European legislation.

The Council of Ministers

This is made up of one representative from each of the 15 member states. As the representative must be a government minister, this means that the appropriate minister responsible for the topic under discussion can attend, e.g. for farming matters, the minister for rural affairs. The presidency is taken on a rotational basis by each member state for a 6-month period. The Council has to ensure the treaty objectives are reached and it has a role in making EU legislation. It can initiate legislation but, in most cases, it only acts on proposals from the Commission. However, it does have the final say.

The Council reaches its decisions by voting on the matters under discussion. The 87 votes are divided among the member states in proportion to the size of their population. The necessary vote may take the form of a simple majority in favour of the proposal, a unanimous decision with all members voting for the proposal, as in taxation matters, or a qualified majority of 62 votes in favour. A member state can exercise a right of veto in cases where it is considered that important national interests are involved.

The Commission

The 20 Commissioners are appointed by each member state for a period of 5 years. They are required to be independent and represent the interests of the EU rather than those of their own countries. The Commission acts as the executive body of the EU, initiating and coordinating EU policy. It is involved in both making and enforcing EU law. It presents its proposals and draft legislation to the Council to be discussed and voted on. It also has the power to pass certain types of delegated legislation which forms the bulk of EU legislation. The enforcement role allows it to intervene if a member state has not implemented EU law, and it can refer cases to the European Court of Justice. The president of the Commission is appointed by heads of government.

The European Parliament

This is made up of 626 members directly elected by their own countries every 5 years. The members form political groups rather than national ones. It supervises the work of the Commission and has the right of veto over the annual budget proposals. Unlike the UK, the European Parliament does not form the legislature. It cannot propose legislation but it still has a part to play in the legislative process. Originally, it only had a consultative and supervisory role, but this has been enhanced over the years, especially in the Treaty of Maastricht (EU Treaty) 1992.

The process of making European Union Law

Under the EC Treaty there is no single legislative body or procedure. The Commission proposes legislation. Some areas only require a proposal from the Commission and the approval of the Council; however, the Parliament is usually consulted — this is the **consultation procedure**.

Other areas of legislation require Parliament's assent before the Council's approval is given. Two new procedures, the **cooperation procedure**, introduced by the Single European Act 1986, and the **co-decision procedure**, introduced by the Maastricht Treaty, give the Parliament a greater role in making EU legislation.

Both procedures start with the Commission's proposals being considered by the Council and the Parliament. Parliament's opinions are considered by the Council members, who reach a common position. The legislation is then referred back to the Parliament which can approve the Council's common position, amend the common position or reject it. This is the second reading stage. The two latter options require an absolute majority from the Parliament. If Parliament rejects the common position, the proposal may still be adopted if the Council agrees unanimously to do so. If Parliament amends the common position, the proposal is referred back to the Commission so that the amendments can be included in a revised proposal. This goes back to the Commission for its acceptance or rejection. A qualified majority is needed for this.

The co-decision procedure introduced a third reading stage. If this procedure is being used and no agreement is reached after the second reading stage, a Conciliation Committee, consisting of members of the Council and the Parliament, is formed to work towards a joint decision. If no decision is reached at this stage, then Parliament has an effective veto because even a unanimous vote by the Council cannot override Parliament.

The European Court of Justice

The European Court of Justice (ECJ) sits in Luxembourg and consists of 15 judges, one from each member state, one of whom is president. They are assisted by eight advocates general. The ECJ's primary function is to 'ensure that in the interpretation and application of this Treaty the law is observed' (Article 220 of the Treaty of Rome).

The ECJ has both a judicial and a supervisory role. When carrying out the judicial role, the ECJ hears cases involving member states or European legislation. The Commission may bring a case if a member state has breached community laws. In *Re Tachographs: EC Commission v UK* (1979), the UK had failed to implement a regulation which made it compulsory to fit tachographs in lorries.

The ECJ also hears proceedings against EU institutions. Actions may be started by other EU institutions, member states and sometimes by organisations or individual citizens. Using this procedure, the court can review the legality of regulations, directives or decisions. The grounds for this are that:
- the provisions infringe a treaty or a rule relating to its application
- the powers have been misused
- there is a failure to follow the proper procedures

In its supervisory role, the ECJ hears references for preliminary rulings on the interpretation of EU law from national courts. Article 234 of the EU Treaty (formally Article 177 of the Treaty of Rome) allows a reference to be made if the national court considers it necessary to have a decision on the question to enable it to make a judgment. Once a ruling has been made by the ECJ, it is binding on the courts of all the member states.

If there is no further appeal from the particular national court, then a reference must be made from that court to the ECJ, for example from the House of Lords in the UK. In the lower courts referral is discretionary. In *Bulmer* v *Bollinger* (1974) Lord Denning set out guidelines to be used when deciding whether a reference should be made. He said that a reference should only be made if it would be conclusive in the case. No reference should be made if:

- the ECJ had already made a ruling on the same point
- the point in question was reasonably clear and free from doubt

where other matters would remain undecided, a reference would be unnecessary.

Cases where references have been made to the ECJ include *Van Duyn* v *Home Office* (1974) and *Marshall* v *Southampton Area Health Authority* (1986). In *Tarfaen Borough Council* v *B&Q* (1990), Cwmbran Magistrates' Court made a reference to find out if the Sunday trading restrictions, which were in force at that time, were in breach of the Treaty of Rome.

When the court makes a reference to the ECJ, this has the effect of suspending the proceedings in the national court until the verdict is given. The verdict gives an explanation of the European law concerned and the national court makes its decision based on that. The ECJ does not tell the national court what decision to make in the case. In 1988 the Single European Act created a European Court of First Instance in order to reduce the workload of the ECJ.

The effect of EU membership on parliamentary supremacy

The doctrine of parliamentary supremacy means that Parliament has the position of the highest source of law in the UK. Parliament can decide to make whatever law it wishes and the courts must apply that law, no matter how controversial that law is. Parliamentary law takes precedence over law from any other source.

Membership of the EU has had a significant effect on this. The European Communities Act 1972 removes part of this supremacy because in those areas where the EU can make laws, EU law has to take precedence over UK law. The case of *Costa* v *ENEL* (1964) established the fact that a later national law did not take precedence over EU law.

The leading case in the UK which illustrates the fact that EU law must take priority is *R* v *Secretary of State for Transport, ex parte Factortame* (1990). The British government enacted the Merchant Shipping Act 1988 with the aim of preventing Spanish fishermen, who had registered their boats in the UK in order to take advantage of the British fishing quota, from doing so. The Spanish boat owners challenged this on the grounds that it conflicted with EU law on the freedom to set up a business anywhere in the EU. The House of Lords said that this was right and the Merchant Shipping Act could not be enforced. This means that the courts can refuse to apply statutes which conflict with directly effective EU law.

The principles of direct applicability and direct effect for treaty articles and regulations further erode this principle. This was seen in the Tachograph case, where the UK was taken before the ECJ for its failure to implement the regulation. The principles also allow citizens to enforce their rights even if they have not specifically been enacted as part of UK law, in the case of treaty articles, or not implemented/implemented defectively, in the case of directives.

Other people argue that membership of the EU has not affected parliamentary supremacy. Parliament is still the supreme law-making body in those areas not covered by EU law. Parliament's supremacy has been suspended on a limited and temporary basis, although for an unlimited period, because Parliament retains a residual power under s.2(4) of the European Communities Act 1972 to repeal or amend s.2 in order to return to full supremacy.

Statute law

UK legislation, which consists of Acts of Parliament (statutes), is the result of a process involving the House of Commons, the House of Lords, which together form Parliament, and the monarch (Queen Elizabeth II). The statutes are primary legislation. The House of Commons is made up of members of Parliament (MPs) elected by local people to represent their individual constituencies. The political party holding the majority of seats forms the government of the day. The House of Lords, whose members are unelected (at the present time), consists of 92 hereditary peers (elected by their fellow peers) with the rest of the House being life peers appointed by the government, Law Lords and senior bishops.

How statutes are created

Bills

Every Act of Parliament begins life as a bill, which is a draft law, and may fall into one of three categories:
- public bills
- private bills
- private member's bills

Public bills

These are the most common type. They have general effect and are concerned with public policy affecting the law of the country, e.g. Access to Justice Act 1999. The major bills are outlined in the Queen's speech and are usually introduced in Parliament by the minister concerned.

Before a bill is drawn up, the government department involved in the proposed changes to the law may issue a consultative document — a **Green Paper** — setting out the proposals and allowing interested parties to comment on them. Any necessary changes can then be made and the final proposals are set out in a **White Paper**. The bill is drawn up by parliamentary counsel (specialist lawyers in drafting bills) on the instructions of the relevant government department. They aim to make sure that the proposed law will be exactly as intended, but this is not always successful and may result in the need for statutory interpretation at a later date.

Private bills

This type of bill is one in which the provisions only apply to part of the community. They are usually concerned with matters of a local nature and are promoted by bodies, such as local authorities or statutory bodies, which are seeking special powers.

Private member's bills

These are introduced by backbench MPs whose names have been selected by ballot (20 each year). The choice of subject is the MP's own but, as time for debate on these bills is limited, very few become law. They are introduced during the Friday sittings of the parliamentary session. They can be a way of drawing attention to areas of law where there may be a need for change, and some have been successful. The Abortion Act 1967 resulted from David Steel's private member's bill.

The process of a bill through Parliament

A bill cannot become an Act of Parliament until it has been passed by both Houses of Parliament. The procedure consists of a number of stages, and may commence in either the House of Commons or the House of Lords. However, finance bills must begin in the House of Commons.

First reading

The first reading takes place when the title of the bill is read out to the House and is purely formal.

Second reading

The bill is usually proposed by the government minister responsible for the proposals and this stage allows the House to hold a full debate on the general principles of the bill. At the end of the debate a vote is taken as to whether or not the bill should proceed. If the vote goes against the bill, it can go no further.

Committee stage

If the vote is in favour, the bill passes to the committee stage. A standing committee of MPs from all the political parties carries out a detailed examination of the bill. Every clause in the bill is examined in detail. Amendments may be made at this stage; these are selected by the chairman. This process can take several months.

Report stage

The committee reports back to the House on any amendments which have been made. Members who are not on the standing committee can propose further amendments. These are debated and voted on.

Third reading

The bill, in its final form, including any amendments made at the earlier stages, is presented to the House and the final vote is taken.

Passage through the other House

If the bill was introduced in the House of Commons, it then passes to the House of Lords (or vice versa), where the same procedure is repeated. Further amendments can be made to the bill. In the House of Lords the committee stage is usually a committee of the whole House. There is a line-by-line examination of the whole bill. No selection of amendments takes place, all can be considered and there is unrestricted debate on them. If the House of Lords makes amendments to a bill which has already passed through the House of Commons, it will be referred back to the House of Commons to consider the amendments.

The Royal Assent

Once a bill has successfully passed through all the stages in both Houses, it has to receive the Royal Assent from the Queen. This no longer has to be given in person and the last time it was refused was in 1707. The Royal Assent is usually announced to each House by its speaker. The bill then becomes an Act of Parliament.

The position of the House of Lords

The House of Lords is considered to be a check on the executive's powers (the executive is made up of the prime minister, Cabinet and government ministers), acting as a safeguard against the abuse of power. At times it has made the government rethink its proposals; for example, the home secretary's plans to abolish trial by jury for certain offences was defeated after the House of Lords made amendments to it. Less controversial government bills are introduced in the House of Lords, enlarging the government's legislative output. There is usually no difficulty in these passing through the House of Commons, but a bill which was not acceptable to the House of Commons would not become law.

At one time, the unelected House of Lords was able to prevent legislation put forward by the elected House of Commons, as the agreement of both Houses was necessary. This power is restricted by the Parliament Acts 1911 and 1949. If the House of Lords rejects a bill, provided it is reintroduced to the House of Commons in the next parliamentary session and passes all the stages again, it can become law.

Some Acts of Parliament come into force when the Royal Assent is given, but most commence on a specific date which may be stated in the Act. Sometimes different parts of the Act may come into effect at different times, which can cause uncertainty as it can be difficult to find out which sections are in force.

Usually the legislative process takes several months to complete, especially if the proposals are controversial. On some occasions, however, if all the parties are in agreement that a new law is needed urgently, an Act may be passed in 24 hours, for example the Northern Ireland Bill 1972.

One problem with the legislative process is the way in which the original proposals in a bill can be amended, often more than once. This can result in the final legislation being unclear in some areas and having to be interpreted by the courts in the future.

The doctrine of parliamentary supremacy

Parliamentary supremacy (sovereignty) is a fundamental part of the UK constitution. As Parliament is a democratically elected body, it should make all the laws of the country. This means that Acts of Parliament that have been passed using the proper procedures cannot be challenged. They must be applied by the courts and override any judicial precedent, delegated legislation or previous Act of Parliament which covers that area of law. Parliament also has the power to rescind (unmake) any law which it has passed.

Some limitations on Parliament's supremacy have resulted from the UK joining the European Community in 1973. Under the Treaty of Rome 1957, European Community law, enacted by the powers set out in the treaties, takes priority over conflicting laws in member states. The European Communities Act 1972 incorporates this principle into UK law. Even if Parliament passes an Act which conflicts with EU law, EU law must prevail, as shown in the *Factortame* case in 1990. For areas of law not covered by the EU, Parliament is supreme.

The Human Rights Act 1998, which came into force in October 2000, incorporates the European Convention on Human Rights into English law. Under this Act the Convention does not have superiority over English law and Parliament can still make laws that conflict with it. However, under s.19 of the Act, all bills require a statement from a government minister before the second reading in each House, saying that the provisions of the bill are compatible with the Convention, or, if not, that the government intends the bill to proceed. If the courts find a provision in a statute which breaches the Convention then, under s.10 of the 1998 Act, the appropriate minister can amend this by an Order in Council. Normally this would be done by another Act of Parliament, but the minister is not obliged to change the law. Consequently, the Human Rights Act only has a slight effect on parliamentary supremacy.

Delegated legislation

Delegated legislation (secondary legislation) is law that is authorised but not made by Parliament. Parliament may create a framework of law, in many cases in a statute. This type of statute is known as an **enabling Act** and other people or bodies are delegated powers to make the more detailed rules required. More delegated legislation is made each year than statute law.

Types of delegated legislation

Delegated legislation can be one of three types: Orders in Council, statutory instruments and bylaws.

Orders in Council

Orders in Council are used when it would be inappropriate to use a statutory instrument, for example when transferring responsibilities between government departments. The powers of the ministers in the UK government were transferred to the ministers of the devolved assemblies using Orders in Council (Scotland Act 1998 (Transfer of Functions to the Scottish Ministers Etc. Order 1999). Orders in Council are made by the Privy Council. They often relate to the regulation of professional bodies or professions.

In times of emergency, when Parliament is not sitting, under the Emergency Powers Act 1920, the Queen and Privy Council may make an Order in Council. The government can also use this method in times of emergency, for example the fuel crisis of 2000.

Statutory instruments

This is the most common type of delegated legislation. There were 3,299 statutory instruments made in 2002. Authority is given under the enabling Act for ministers and government departments to make these. The legal department of the ministry concerned usually drafts them. They cover many areas including road traffic regulations and health and safety at work.

Bylaws

Parliament has given local authorities and other public bodies the right to make the law in certain areas. Local authorities, for example county councils, district councils and parish councils, can make bylaws to cover such things as parking restrictions and banning the drinking of alcohol in certain public places. Public bodies can also make bylaws to help to enforce rules concerning public behaviour, such as the ban on smoking on the London Underground. All bylaws must be approved by the relevant government minister.

Control of delegated legislation

As most delegated legislation is not made by elected bodies and many people have the power to create it, it is important to ensure that the power is not abused and is controlled. This can be done by Parliament or the courts.

Control by Parliament

Parliament has limited control at the time an enabling Act is made, as it sets the parameters for making delegated legislation under that Act. In addition, the **Delegated Powers Scrutiny Committee** in the House of Lords can decide whether the provisions in a bill to delegate legislative power are inappropriate. The committee examines all bills which contain delegated powers before they start their passage through the House of Lords. Its report is presented to the House of Lords before the committee stage but it has no power to amend the bill.

Some enabling Acts require an **affirmative resolution** from Parliament before the delegated legislation can become law. The delegated legislation has to be laid before both Houses and, if a vote approving it is taken within a specified time, it becomes law.

Much more delegated legislation is subject to a **negative resolution**. The delegated legislation is put before Parliament and, if no member has put down a motion to annul it within a specified period (usually 40 days), it becomes law.

The **Joint Committee on Statutory Instruments**, with members from both Houses of Parliament (the Scrutiny Committee), reviews all statutory instruments and can draw the attention of Parliament to those which need special consideration. A statutory instrument will be referred back to Parliament if:

- it imposes a tax
- under the Act the statutory instrument cannot be challenged in the courts
- the delegated legislation appears to be retrospectively effective and was not provided for in the enabling Act
- the powers granted in the Act have been exceeded or used in an unusual way
- the legislation is defective or needs clarification

The committee has no power to alter the legislation — it merely reports back on its findings — but it does provide a check on delegated legislation. Parliament itself holds the ultimate safeguard, in that it can withdraw the delegated power and revoke any piece of delegated legislation at any time.

Control by the courts

Unlike a statute, the validity of delegated legislation can be challenged in the courts. Any individual who has a personal interest in the delegated legislation, that is, is being affected by it, may apply to the courts under the **judicial review** procedure. The ground for this is that the individual believes that the piece of delegated legislation is *ultra vires* (goes beyond the powers granted by Parliament). If it is found to be *ultra vires*, the delegated legislation is declared void and ineffective.

This can be in the form of **procedural** *ultra vires*, where a public authority has not followed the procedures set out in the enabling Act for creating delegated legislation.

In *Agricultural, Horticultural and Forestry Training Board* v *Aylesbury Mushrooms Ltd* (1972), failure by the minister for labour to consult interested parties led to the order being declared invalid.

A claim of **substantive** *ultra vires* occurs where the delegated legislation goes beyond the powers granted by the enabling Act. In *R* v *Home Secretary, ex parte Fire Brigades Union* (1995), where the home secretary made changes to the Criminal Injuries Compensation Scheme, he was held to have exceeded the power given in the Criminal Justice Act 1988.

The courts will also declare invalid delegated legislation which is unreasonable. This may be because the rules are unjust, made in bad faith or are so perverse that no reasonable person would have made them, as stated in *Wednesbury Corporation* v *ABC Cinemas*.

The effectiveness of the controls on delegated legislation

There are drawbacks to control by Parliament. The use of the affirmative procedure usually draws Parliament's attention to the delegated legislation, but rarely can it stop the legislation from being passed. The Scrutiny Committee is more important and has managed to have changes made to some pieces of delegated legislation. However, the Committee does lack power because it can only consider whether the delegated powers have been used correctly, and not the merits of the legislation. Its reports are not binding either.

Control by the courts has been successful in many cases, but even this has problems. The delegated legislation may have been in force for years before someone affected by it is prepared to challenge it. Another problem is that the discretionary powers conferred on the minister by the enabling Act may be extremely wide, resulting in difficulties in establishing that he or she has acted *ultra vires*.

The necessity for delegated legislation

There are a number of reasons why delegated legislation is needed:
- There is not enough time for Parliament to consider every detail of regulations/rules.
- Parliament does not have the knowledge or technical expertise necessary in certain areas, e.g. building regulations, health and safety regulations at work. Delegated legislation allows experts in the relevant areas to make the rules.

- Local knowledge is very important for local authorities to make effective bylaws.
- Delegated legislation can be achieved more quickly than an Act of Parliament. This also allows flexibility, as delegated legislation can be amended more quickly if circumstances change.
- Delegated legislation can be easily revoked if it causes problems. An Act of Parliament would require another statute to amend or revoke it, which takes much longer.
- It is impossible for Parliament to foresee all the problems which could arise when passing a statute. When problems do arise, delegated legislation to rectify this can be put into place quickly.

Disadvantages of delegated legislation

The main argument against delegated legislation is that it is undemocratic because it is made by unelected people rather than by Parliament. Much of the delegated legislation is sub-delegated and made by civil servants in the relevant government departments rather than by the ministers who were given the original delegated powers. This is not the case with bylaws, as local authorities are elected bodies and accountable to the voters in their area.

The large amount of delegated legislation makes it difficult to keep track of the current law. It receives little publicity compared with that received by Acts of Parliament, so people may be unaware that a particular piece of legislation exists.

Influences on Parliament

As the major legislative body, Parliament can be influenced by political pressures, law reform agencies, pressure groups, public opinion and the media.

Political pressures

When a general election is to be held, each political party presents a **party manifesto** setting out the proposals which it will make law if elected to government. These have covered such things as the right to buy council houses, the Housing Act 1980 and the poll tax.

Membership of the EU is another influence, as it creates obligations under the treaties whereby decisions made by the EU Commission or Council of Ministers are enacted as new laws.

Civil servants in each ministerial department also have their own views about the legislation necessary to achieve their goals.

Law reform agencies

These include the Law Commission and, on occasions, Royal Commissions.

The Law Commission

The Law Commission was established by the Law Commission Act 1965. It is a full-time body with five law commissioners. The chairman is a High Court judge and the other four are either from the legal professions or are academic lawyers. Their staff is all legally trained. The Commission's work involves looking at reform of the law, codification and consolidation. It may have topics referred to it by the Lord Chancellor and government departments, or select a topic of its own, which will be considered after gaining government approval.

After researching a selected area of law, the Commission produces a consultative paper which details the present law, setting out the problems and options for change. The views of interested parties are sought, after which a final report is published, setting out its recommendations and, if legislation is proposed, a draft bill. This only becomes law if it goes through the parliamentary process described on pp. 16–17. Legislation which has resulted from this process includes the Law Reform (Year and a Day Rule) Act 1996 and the Contract (Rights of Third Parties) Act 1999.

The success rate of the Law Commission in the area of law reform has varied. Initially, the Law Commission had a high success rate with its proposals being accepted and enacted, but this has not been maintained. The Commission has made over 100 proposals of which about 70% have been adopted.

Another of the original aims of the Law Commission was to codify the law in certain areas. This has not come about. The Draft Criminal Code was published in 1985 but has never become law. The arguments in favour of codification are that it makes the law accessible and understandable, and provides consistency and certainty. People then know what the law is, as it is contained in one place. What the Commission has done in this area is to select areas of law and clarify these, hoping to codify them at a later date, if possible.

Consolidation involves drawing together all the provisions set out in a number of statutes so that they are all in one Act. The Law Commission carries out this process and about five consolidation bills are produced each year. A problem with this is that, even when the area of law is consolidated, further Acts of Parliament may change it again. The Powers of the Criminal Courts (Sentencing) Act 2000 was changed by the Criminal Justice and Courts Act 2000, where community sentences were renamed and new powers of sentencing created.

Royal Commissions

Royal Commissions are temporary committees set up to review a specific area of law. They are usually referred to by the name of their chairman, e.g. the Royal Commission on Criminal Justice 1993 was known as the Runciman Commission. Their job is complete when they have made their report. Commission members are usually drawn from a cross-section of people with expertise in the subject concerned. A Royal Commission can have research carried out on its behalf and interested parties can make submissions. The final report details its recommendations but the government does not have to act on them.

Important changes to the law have resulted from Royal Commissions. The Police and Criminal Evidence Act 1984 was the result of the Royal Commission on Police Procedure (Phillips Commission 1981). The Criminal Appeal Act 1995 and the Criminal Procedure and Investigation Act 1996 both resulted from the Runciman Commission 1993 on criminal justice.

Pressure groups

Pressure groups are bodies of people with a shared interest in getting the government to change the law in certain areas. They include groups such as Shelter, Help the Aged, Greenpeace, Friends of the Earth, trade unions, business groups (e.g. the Confederation of British Industry), and professional organisations such as the Law Society. The goal of some pressure groups is to get their aims onto the legislative agenda. Other groups adopt moral campaigns, for example the National Viewers and Listeners Organisation, which was inspired by Mary Whitehouse.

Pressure groups target politicians, civil servants and local government offices by lobbying MPs, organising petitions and gaining as much publicity as possible for their causes. Well-organised groups, such as Greenpeace and Friends of the Earth, have been highly successful. Governments now have to consider the environmental impact of their policies because of heightened public awareness of environmental issues. Shelter was successful in persuading the government to introduce change for homeless people in the Housing Homeless Persons Act 1977. At times groups may join forces to get their point across to the government. This happened in September 2002 when those people opposed to the banning of fox hunting held a joint march in London with the Countryside Alliance.

Large pressure groups are often more successful than smaller ones, although sometimes one person can bring about change almost single-handed. The late Mary Whitehouse, for example, led a campaign against child pornography which resulted in the government introducing the Protection of Children Act 1978.

Some pressure groups only exist for a short time as they are set up to deal with a specific issue, for example a campaign about a proposed bypass. The group will disband once the issue is resolved.

Sometimes pressure groups are set up as the result of a tragic event, such as the Dunblane massacre in 1996. The Snowdrop Petition organised after the event resulted in Parliament banning the private ownership of most types of hand guns.

However, even if an interest or pressure group does manage to present its arguments, this does not mean that its views will be taken into consideration.

Pressure groups are considered beneficial to the legislative process. They inform the legislature of the need for new legislation and what form it should take. This leads to a more efficient and effective process. Pressure groups inform and stimulate public debate. They empower the weaker groups in society by bringing people together and involving them in the process, thereby making it democratic.

On the other hand, because some small groups are well organised and well resourced, they are more influential than their size and level of support in the society as a whole would suggest. There has also been a growth in professional lobbying agencies, which leads to concern that pressure group activity might distort the democratic process.

Public opinion

Individuals can make their views known by writing to newspapers, their MPs and ministers. If the government has a small majority or if it is coming towards the end of its term of office, it is more likely to consider making reforms.

The media

The media plays a powerful role in bringing issues to the attention of the government. By giving an issue plenty of coverage in the newspapers and on television and radio, it can be brought to the notice of the public and add weight to public opinion. The problem with this is that, in some cases, the media whip up public opinion instead of reflecting it.

Statutory interpretation

The process of statutory interpretation is used by judges in the courts when there is a dispute or uncertainty over the meaning of a word or phrase in an Act of Parliament or piece of delegated legislation. The role of the courts is to find out how Parliament intended the law to apply and carry this out. This interpretation may form a precedent for future cases. The necessity for this can arise for a number of reasons:

- Due to the complexity of the English language a word may have several meanings, which can lead to ambiguity.

- The meaning of words can change over time.
- The legislation may have been drawn up very quickly in response to public reaction and the wording may not be as precise as it should be, for example the Dangerous Dogs Act 1991.
- The original bill may contain errors in the drafting. Parliament may not notice this, especially if there are many amendments during the bill's passage through all its parliamentary stages.
- Changes in technology and social issues can affect how an Act is applied, for example the *Royal College of Nursing* v *DHSS* (1981).
- The amount of delegated legislation is increasing.

Approaches to interpretation

Judges can use three main '**rules**' or **canons of construction** in interpreting Acts of Parliament:
- the literal rule
- the golden rule
- the mischief rule

These are not rules as such but different ways of approaching the interpretation of a statute. Each individual judge decides which particular 'rule' to use in any particular case.

The literal rule

The assumption here is that the best way to determine the intention of Parliament, when interpreting a statute, is to give the words used their literal or ordinary meaning even if this produces an absurd result.

The literal rule was used in *Whiteley* v *Chappell* (1868), where the defendant was charged with the offence of impersonating 'any person entitled to vote' at an election. The defendant was acquitted because he impersonated a dead person who was not entitled to vote!

In *Fisher* v *Bell* (1961), a shopkeeper put flick-knives on display in his window. The Restriction of Offensive Weapons Act 1959 made it an offence to sell flick-knives or offer them for sale. The court decided that, in Contract Law, flick-knives on show in a shop window were not an offer to sell the knives but an invitation for people to make an offer to buy the knives, an 'invitation to treat'. Despite the Act being designed to prevent this type of display, the defendant was not guilty of an offence. Parliament had to change the Act as a result of this case.

This rule has also led to unfair and harsh decisions. For example, in *London & North Eastern Railway Co* v *Berriman* (1946), Mrs Berriman was unable to obtain any compensation because her husband, who was killed while carrying out maintenance work —

oiling points on the railway line — was not engaged in 'relaying or repairing' it, which required a lookout to be provided to warn the rail workers of approaching trains. The words 'relaying' and 'repairing' were given their literal meaning.

The advantage of the literal rule is that law making is left to the elected members, so maintaining parliamentary sovereignty. A disadvantage is that even where the courts use a dictionary to determine the meaning of the words in question, there may be a number of alternative meanings. The rule does not work when the words in the statute do not provide the answer to the problem. The rule also assumes that words can be given plain, ordinary meanings without considering them in context. There have been cases where the judges agreed on the use of the literal rule, but then interpreted the words in different ways, for example *Liversidge* v *Anderson* (1942) and *LNER* v *Berriman* (1946).

Professor Michael Zander QC, Emeritus Professor of Law at the London School of Economics and author of *The Law Making Process*, considers the literal rule to be 'mechanical and divorced from the realities of the use of language'.

The golden rule

The golden rule came about in the case of *Mattison* v *Hart* in the nineteenth century. It allows a different approach to be adopted. The judge starts by looking at the literal meaning but, if there is an ambiguity which would produce an absurdity or injustice, the judge may interpret the Act so as to avoid this.

This rule was used in *R* v *Allen* (1872). Section 57 of the Offences Against the Person Act 1861 stated that if a married person whose husband or wife was still living, married someone else, he or she had committed the offence of bigamy. However, it is impossible for a person who is in an existing marriage to legally marry someone else. Any further marriage would be void. Using the literal rule would mean that it was impossible to commit the offence of bigamy. The court used the golden rule and held that 'marry' meant to go through a ceremony of marriage. Allen was convicted. In *Adler* v *George* (1964), the Official Secrets Act 1920 s.3 made it an offence to be found 'in the vicinity of a prohibited place'. The accused was arrested inside the prohibited place and so argued that he could not be convicted. Lord Parker CJ used the golden rule and held that 'in the vicinity of' could mean 'being in or in the vicinity of the prohibited place'.

The golden rule has also been used where the words have one clear meaning but this would lead to a repugnant situation. The use of the rule allows the court to avoid the problem. This happened in the case of *Re Sigsworth* (1935). A son who murdered his mother was prevented from inheriting his mother's estate under the intestacy rules set out in the Administration of Estates Act 1925. The wording of the Act was unambiguous, but the court did not want the murderer to benefit from his crime.

The advantage of the golden rule is that it can prevent the injustice and absurdity caused as a result of using the literal rule. However, Zander describes it as 'little more than a safety valve' which allows the courts to avoid some of the worst effects of the literal rule. He does not regard it 'as a sound basis for judicial decision making'.

The mischief rule

The mischief rule was laid down in *Heydon's Case* (1584). Judges should consider three factors when using this rule:
- What was the common law before the Act was passed?
- What was the problem with that law?
- What was the remedy that Parliament was trying to provide?

The judge should look for the 'mischief' the Act was designed to remedy and interpret it in such a way as to achieve this. This may mean disregarding the other two rules.

The mischief rule was used in *Smith* v *Hughes* (1960) where 'soliciting in the street' in the Street Offences Act 1958 was held to include soliciting from the window of a house. The court said that the aim of the Act was to allow people to walk along the streets without being solicited, and it should be interpreted to cover this situation. In *Royal College of Nursing* v *DHSS* (1981) the court had to consider the wording of the Abortion Act 1967. The House of Lords looked at the mischief that Parliament was aiming to redress — illegal, 'backstreet abortions' — and decided that nurses supervising part of the procedure was not unlawful because the procedure in question was carried out under the instructions of a doctor in hygienic conditions.

There are limitations on the use of the mischief rule. In *Jones* v *Wrotham Park* (1980) Lord Diplock said that it could only be used where:
- the mischief could clearly be seen from the Act
- it is apparent that Parliament has overlooked the particular problem
- additional words required can be stated with a high degree of certainty

The mischief rule has the advantage of avoiding absurdity and injustice and promoting flexibility. In 1969 the Law Commission described it as a 'rather more satisfactory approach' than the other two rules. The disadvantages are based on the fact that at the time *Heydon's Case* was decided, statutes were a minor source of law, unlike today. The supremacy of Parliament was not so well established and judges were involved in drafting statutes on behalf of the King, which Parliament passed as a mere formality. Therefore, since the legislative process is so different today, the rule may be less appropriate now.

The purposive approach

The first two rules discussed involve judges taking a literal approach to interpreting legislation. The mischief rule takes a broader, purposive approach. This has led to debate as to which approach judges should take. Lord Denning, in the Court of Appeal in 1950, believed that judges should take the purposive approach but was unable to persuade the House of Lords. In its report in 1967, the Law Commission recommended the purposive approach as the one to take. Zander also supports this view.

The approach requires the court to examine the object of the Act and to construe doubtful passages in accordance with that purpose. Over the last 20 years, the purposive approach has gained ground. The European Court of Justice uses this approach in interpreting European law and the English courts have to use the same approach when interpreting domestic legislation brought in as a result of this. The Human Rights Act 1998 is also likely to cause a shift towards the purposive approach.

Presumptions

When interpreting an Act the court can make certain presumptions. Where there is doubt or ambiguity, certain things are assumed:
- There is no change in the common law unless there is a clear indication to the contrary.
- *Mens rea* (the mental element/state of mind for the offence) is required in criminal cases. Any ambiguity should be interpreted in favour of the defendant.
- A strict liability offence is not created unless Parliament specifically says so.
- Legislation is not retrospective in its operation — normally an Act only applies from the day it comes into force.
- The Crown is not bound unless the statute specifically states so.

Rules of language

These are common sense rules which have been developed over time. They allow judges to look at other words in the Act in order to make the meaning of words and phrases clear. The rules are:
- *ejusdem generis*: general terms which follow specific ones are taken to include only things of the same kind. If an Act uses the phrase 'dogs, cats and other animals', the 'other animals' would include other domestic animals but not wild animals.
- *expressio unius est exclusio alterius*: express mention of one thing implies the exclusion of another. If an Act specifically refers to Labrador dogs, it would not include other breeds of dog.
- *noscitur a sociis*: a word draws meaning from other words around it. Where an Act deals with houses 'for public refreshment, resort and entertainment', the last word is held not to cover theatrical or musical entertainment, but to refer to refreshment rooms and the reception and accommodation of the public.

Aids to statutory interpretation

There are various aids which judges can use when interpreting a statute. These include:

- internal or intrinsic aids
- external or extrinsic aids

Internal or intrinsic aids

These are found in other parts of the Act itself and may help to make its meaning clear. These aids include:

- the long title and the short title of the Act
- the preamble, if there is one
- the interpretation section
- headings before any sections or groups of sections
- schedules
- punctuation
- purpose section — The Children Act 1989: 'the child's welfare shall be the court's paramount consideration'

External or extrinsic aids

These are matters found outside the Act and include:

- dictionaries of the time
- the historical setting
- previous Acts of Parliament on the same subject matter
- earlier case law
- reference to Hansard, the official report of the proceedings in Parliament. Until 1990, the courts were not allowed to refer to Hansard in order to find out Parliament's intention. This rule was overturned in *Pepper* v *Hart* (1993). However, this use is restricted to cases where the words of an Act are ambiguous or obscure or lead to an absurdity but, even then, only if there is a clear statement by the minister introducing the legislation which would resolve this. The wider use of Hansard is only permitted if the legislation in question has introduced an inter-national convention or European directive into English Law.
- law reform reports from bodies such as the Law Commission
- international treaties. *Fothergill* v *Monarch Airlines Ltd* (1980) confirmed that *travaux preparatoires* (background working papers) could be used to ascertain the meaning of an ambiguous or doubtful section of an Act which was based on an international treaty.
- explanatory notes. All Acts passed since the beginning of 1999 have explanatory notes which are published at the same time as the new bill.

Judicial precedent

When the facts of a case are similar to one which has already been decided, the judge must follow that previous decision, especially if it was reached by a higher court. This forms the basis of judicial precedent and is known as *stare decisis* (let the decision stand).

After hearing a case, when a judge presents his written judgment, this is known as **case law**. This judgment sets out the facts of the case and the legal principles which he has used to reach his decision. The legal principles are known as the *ratio decidendi* (the reason for deciding). This is the **binding precedent** which forms the case law if the court where the case was heard is one in which the judge is bound by the court's previous decisions. Examples of *ratio decidendi* are the 'neighbour' principle in *Donoghue* v *Stevenson* (1932) and the rule in *R* v *Nedrick* (1986), confirmed in *R* v *Woollin* (1997), that if a jury considers that the defendant foresaw death or serious injury as a virtual certainty, oblique intention may be inferred.

Not all of a judgment forms the *ratio decidendi*. Sometimes the judge may say what the decision might have been if the situation were different. This is known as *obiter dicta* (things said by the way). Although this is not part of the case law, it may influence judges in later cases as **persuasive precedent**. Lord Denning's *obiter dicta* statements in the case of *Central London Property Trust Ltd* v *High Trees House Ltd* (1947) led to the creation of the doctrine of *promissory estoppel*.

Persuasive precedent may also arise from the lower courts. The House of Lords agreed with the reasons that the Court of Appeal gave in the case of *R* v *R* (1991) when deciding that a man could be found guilty of raping his wife.

When a court reaches a majority decision (in the Court of Appeal a case is usually heard by three judges, in the House of Lords by five) the dissenting judge(s) have to give their reasons for dissenting. If the case goes to appeal in a higher court, these reasons may be followed as persuasive precedent if the higher court disagrees with the majority decision of the lower court.

Decisions of the Judicial Committee of the Privy Council (JCPC) (many of the judges in the court are members of the House of Lords and therefore very senior judges) are made as a result of their role as a court of final appeal for some Commonwealth countries. These decisions are not binding on the English courts but they can form persuasive precedent. The Court of Appeal in *Doughty* v *Turner Manufacturing Co Ltd* (1964) chose to follow the JCPC decision, involving liability and remoteness of damage in the tort of negligence, in the *Wagon Mound No 1* (1961), rather than its own earlier decision in *Re Polemis* (1921).

Sometimes the decisions of courts in the other Commonwealth countries such as Canada, Australia and New Zealand become persuasive precedent.

The hierarchy of the courts

In order for the system of judicial precedent to work, there must be rules for judges to follow to make sure that there is consistency in the law. One way of doing this is to have a system of hierarchy where decisions in the higher courts bind the lower courts. Some of the courts are also bound by their own previous decisions. The system in England is described below.

The European Court of Justice

On matters of EU law (e.g. interpretation of treaties etc.), decisions made by the European Court of Justice (ECJ) are binding on all courts in the UK since it joined the European Community in 1973. The ECJ is not bound by its own previous decisions and can overrule them.

The House of Lords

The House of Lords is bound by the decisions of the ECJ, but as the highest appeal court, its decisions bind all the other English courts. Originally, except where a decision was made *per incuriam* (in error), the House of Lords was bound by its own previous decisions. This was established in *London Street Tramways* v *London County Council* (1898), the reason being to ensure certainty in the law. However, in 1966 the Lord Chancellor issued a Practice Statement which stated that the use of precedent was essential when deciding the law and applying it to individual cases because it provided a degree of certainty which could be relied on. However, the Law Lords recognised that by keeping too rigidly to precedent, injustice might occur and development of the law might be restricted. Therefore, although the decisions of the House of Lords were normally binding, they would depart from their decisions if it appeared right to do so. This would only apply to the House of Lords.

This was seen as an important event but in the years since that decision, the House of Lords has used the power sparingly. It has used its power to overrule its own previous decisions in the following cases:
- *British Railways Board* v *Herrington* (1972) overruled *Addie* v *Dumbreck* (1929) on the duty of care owed to a child trespasser.
- *Murphy* v *Brentwood District Council* (1990) overruled *Anns* v *Merton London Borough Council* (1977) on the duty of care owed by local authorities.
- *Pepper* v *Hart* (1993) overruled the House of Lords' previous decision in *Davis* v *Johnson* (1978), which banned the use of Hansard in statutory interpretation.
- *R* v *Howe* (1987) overruled *R* v *Lynch* (1975) and said that duress was no defence to a murder charge.
- *R* v *Shivpuri* (1987) overruled *Anderton* v *Ryan* (1985) on attempting the impossible in theft.

The Court of Appeal

This Court is divided into two divisions which deal solely with either civil cases or criminal cases. Both are bound by decisions of the House of Lords and the ECJ, but the decisions of one division do not bind the other.

The Court of Appeal (Civil Division)

This division of the Court of Appeal is bound by its own previous decisions. The case of *Young* v *Bristol Aeroplane Co Ltd* (1944) set out three exceptions when the civil division can depart from its own previous decisions. These are:

- the previous decision was made *per incuriam*, for example the decision was made without considering a relevant Act of Parliament
- there are two decisions which conflict
- a later decision of the House of Lords overrules a previous decision in the Court of Appeal

There was a period in the recent past when the Court of Appeal tried to argue that the Practice Statement should also apply to it, but in *Davis* v *Johnson* (1978) the House of Lords reaffirmed that the Court of Appeal was bound by its own previous provisions with the exceptions in *Young's* case.

The Court of Appeal (Criminal Division)

This division is usually bound by its own previous decisions, but may take a more flexible approach if the liberty of an individual is involved. This was upheld in *R* v *Spencer* (1985). The exceptions in *Young's* case also apply.

The High Court

The divisional courts and the ordinary High Court are all bound by the decisions of the Court of Appeal, House of Lords and the ECJ. The Family Division and the Chancery Division (civil courts) are bound by their own previous decisions. There is more flexibility in the Queen's Bench Division when hearing appeals on criminal cases. The ordinary High Court is bound by the decisions of the divisional courts but not by its own previous decisions, although it is generally accepted that these, if reported, have persuasive authority.

The crown court

This court is bound by the decisions of all the higher courts. Its decisions are not binding precedent but the decisions of High Court judges sitting in the crown court form persuasive precedent. The court is not bound to follow its own decisions.

Magistrates' courts and county courts

These courts are bound by the courts above them but their own decisions do not form binding or persuasive precedent. They are not bound by their own previous decisions.

Law reporting

For the doctrine of judicial precedent to work properly there must be some way in which judges can find out if there are binding precedents in existence. This is achieved by an accurate record of law reporting. There are records going back to around 1275, but the Incorporated Council of Law Reporting was set up in 1865. At present there is a well-established system of reporting, including the *All England Law Reports*, *Weekly Law Reports* and reports published in newspapers such as *The Times*.

How judges avoid following precedent

When deciding a case where there appears to be a precedent set, either by the court hearing the case or a higher court, if the facts are similar to a decided case, the courts must follow the precedent and apply the law in the same way. There are, however, several approaches which judges can take in order to avoid following precedent.

Distinguishing

If the judge finds the facts of a case are sufficiently different from the case setting the precedent, he or she can distinguish the two cases and avoid following precedent. In *King* v *Phillips* (1953) the Court of Appeal said that a mother who suffered shock after seeing the child's tricycle under a taxi and hearing the child scream was not owed a duty of care as the child was not injured in any way. In *Boardman* v *Sanderson* (1964), the claimant's son was injured when the defendant negligently backed his car, the plaintiff was close by, heard the screams and suffered from shock. The claimant was able to recover damages.

Overruling

Judges in the higher courts can overrule the decisions of the lower courts if they consider the legal principles to be wrong. The 1966 Practice Statement allows the House of Lords to depart from its own previous decisions, although it has rarely done so.

It has to be borne in mind that it is the judge in a later case who decides which legal principles are the *ratio decidendi* in the case being considered as the precedent. If more than one judge has given a written judgment in that case, there may be several different *ratios* for the judge to consider. This allows different judges to be able to interpret the judgments in the previous cases quite differently. This can lead either to a narrow interpretation of the *ratio*, restricting it to that particular case, or to a wider one so that it covers the case in question. In some cases the *ratio* cannot be distinguished from the *obiter dicta* and therefore there is no clear *ratio* to follow.

Reversing

Where a case goes to a higher court on appeal, if it considers the law to be wrongly interpreted it may reverse the decision.

The advantages and disadvantages of judicial precedent

Advantages

Certainty and consistency

Certainty allows people to know what the law is and lawyers are able to predict the likely outcome of a case. This may result in a case being settled out of court. Consistency occurs because similar cases are dealt with in the same way.

Flexibility

Flexibility arises through the use of overruling and distinguishing, which allow the law to change. Changes in the attitude of society can also be taken into account, an example being *R* v *R* (1991) when the House of Lords accepted that a man could be guilty of raping his wife.

Precision

Precision arises because the statement of law always relates to the precise facts of the case, leading to detailed practical rules.

Disadvantages

Complexity and volume

There is a large number of reported cases which is continually growing. This makes it difficult to know all of the cases which might be relevant. The judges in each case may only be aware of those which each of the parties concerned bring to their attention. In some cases there is also the difficulty of determining the *ratio decidendi* because of the way in which they are written.

Rigidity

The strict hierarchy means that judges have to follow binding precedent. This means that bad or inappropriate decisions cannot be changed unless they are heard in a higher court which can overrule them.

Unsystematic development

Because of the way case law operates, if a whole series of rules is based on one case which is later overruled, this can cause problems.

Illogical distinctions

The use of distinguishing in order to avoid precedent has led to complexity in some areas of law. There may be only minute differences in some cases which appear illogical. Too many distinctions of this type can lead to unpredictability.

Lack of democracy

When deciding cases in this way judges are actually making law which, under the doctrine of the Separation of Powers, is not part of their role.

Lack of research

Judges are only presented with the facts of the case and any legal arguments in order to decide the case. Unlike Parliament, they cannot commission research on the implications of their decisions.

Retrospective effect

Unlike legislation, which only applies to events after it has come into effect, case law applies retrospectively to events which occurred before the case was brought. This could lead to unfairness if, as a result of the case, the law is changed, because the parties to the case could not have known what the law was prior to their actions.

Questions
&
Answers

This section of the guide provides you with six questions on the topic of **Law Making** in the style of the AQA unit test. As explained in the introduction to this guide, each question is made up of two parts with a total of 30 marks allocated between the two parts. Although the questions are set out in topic areas, it is possible for two topics to be examined in the one question. This is particularly the case with the parliamentary process.

A grade-A candidate response has been provided for every question. Five of the questions also have a grade-C candidate answer. Question 3 has a borderline grade-E response. The grade-A responses are not model answers and should not be learnt parrot fashion. You need to be able to respond to the specific question set, not the question you would like to answer. The answers should be used as a benchmark against which you can compare your own work and discover ways of improving it. The lower grade answers show some of the mistakes students may make.

Examiner's comments

Each answer is accompanied by examiner's comments. These are preceded by the icon **e** and indicate where credit is due. Particular attention is given to the candidate's use of the examinable skills: knowledge and understanding, and analysis and evaluation. In the grade-C answers the examiner points out areas for improvement, specific problems and common errors. The best way to use this section is to attempt the questions without reading the answers first, and then compare your answer with those given.

You are required to write in essay format and, in addition, you will be assessed on your ability to present a coherent, logical argument. Relevant material should be communicated clearly and effectively. Appropriate legal terminology should be used.

Question 1

European law

(a) There are several different types of European law. Describe them,
illustrating your answer with examples where appropriate. *(10 marks)*

(b) Discuss how membership of the European Union has affected English law. *(20 marks)*

■ ■ ■

A-grade answer

(a) When the UK joined the European Community in 1973, the European Communities
Act 1972 was passed by Parliament, so that rights and powers which were created
by or arose under the EC treaties and all such remedies were to be given legal
effect as part of the UK law. This resulted in four new types of law becoming part
of the English law. These are treaties, regulations, directives and decisions.

Treaties are primary sources of law. They are drawn up and ratified by the
heads of the member states. The most important of these is the Treaty of Rome
1957, which created the European Economic Community, established the various
institutions of the EEC and laid down the processes by which further laws —
regulations, directives and decisions — could be passed (Article 249). These are
secondary legislation. As well as setting out the aims of the European Union,
treaties also create some rights and obligations. The type of principles set out in
treaties include men and women who undertake equal pay for work of equal value,
and freedom of movement for workers within the Community.

> ℯ The distinction between primary and secondary legislation is recognised. There are
> also some examples of the type of provision found in treaties.

Regulations are the nearest that EU law comes to an Act of Parliament. They are
used to introduce major changes in EU law which is applicable throughout the
Community. Regulations apply to all member states and usually to people in
general. Regulations are used to set out how some of the treaty articles can be
achieved. The principle of freedom of movement of workers between the member
states is found in the Treaty of Rome. Regulations have made this a reality, giving
the same rights to tax and social advantages as the nationals of that country, for
example housing rights. In *Castelli* v *ONPTS* (1984), a widowed Italian woman who
went to live with her son in Belgium was entitled to receive payment of the guaran-
teed income paid to all old people in Belgium.

Directives are used to bring about harmonisation of systems within the
community. They are addressed to each member state, requiring them to make
changes to their existing law in order to bring it into line with the EU requirements
set out in the directive. In the UK, directives are usually implemented by statutory
instrument. The Unfair Contract Terms Directive was introduced into UK law by
the Unfair Terms in Consumer Contract Regulations 1995.

Decisions are addressed to individual states, organisations or even citizens who are obliged to do whatever is required in the decision. Decisions have been used to deal with situations where Community law has been infringed.

This candidate shows sound understanding of the sources of EU law, explaining the differences between them and using appropriate authority to support the explanations. This answer would be worth 10 marks.

(b) Membership of the EU has had a significant effect on English law. When the UK joined the EEC in 1973, by signing the Treaty of Rome, Parliament had to pass an Act to allow EC law to apply in the UK. The European Communities Act 1972 s.2 establishes that all EC law set out in treaties and regulations, whether already existing or new, is incorporated into UK law. As a result, membership of the EU has affected the doctrine of parliamentary supremacy. Under this doctrine Parliament is the supreme law-making body, having the power to make or unmake any law it wishes to. Any law which has been created using the proper process must be applied by judges and cannot be challenged in the courts. This is based on the fact that Parliament is the democratically elected law-making body. As a result of membership of the EU, in those areas of law which are governed by the EU, Parliament has lost its supremacy. It can no longer make its own laws in those areas. If it does and those laws conflict with existing EU laws, then the national court will not apply that national law.

The candidate shows clear knowledge of how membership of the EU has affected English law. Parliamentary supremacy is explained and the issues surrounding the effects of EU membership on parliamentary supremacy are raised.

Treaty provisions and regulations are directly applicable. This means that in those areas covered by EU law, it is supreme. *Costa* v *ENEL* (1964) established that later national law did not take precedent over existing EU law. If there is an existing piece of domestic legislation which conflicts with EU law, then EU law applies. In *Leonesio* v *Italian Agriculture Minister* (1973) the Italian government had no power to block payments set out in a regulation despite the fact that the Italian Constitution required legislation to authorise government expenditure.

The effect in the UK was tested in *R* v *Secretary of State for Transport, ex parte Factortame* (1990). The Merchant Shipping Act 1988 was intended to protect the fishing quotas of British fishermen from Spanish fishermen who were buying up British boats in order to gain their quota. The regulations passed under the Act said that 75% of a fishing boat had to belong to British citizens. The Spanish fishermen would have been prevented from owning boats and took the issue to the English court. The court sought a ruling from the European Court of Justice on the status of the Act. The ECJ ruled that the Act conflicted with the EU law and should be suspended. The House of Lords refused to apply the Act.

The candidate explains clearly the effect of conflicting laws and the issue of supremacy. Cases have been well selected and used effectively to develop the answer.

The fact that treaty provisions, regulations and some decisions are directly applicable, meaning they take effect immediately in the member states, has also affected parliamentary supremacy. None of these types of EU law requires further legislation to bring them into effect. When a member state ratifies a treaty the provisions automatically become the law of the state. This is direct applicability. The direct applicability of regulations was tested in the Tachograph case when the UK government was found to be in breach of EU law by failing to implement the provision requiring lorry drivers to install tachographs in their cabs. The government left it up to individual drivers to do so.

In *Van Gend en Loos* (1963) it was said that if a treaty provision is unconditional, clear and precise as to the rights and obligations it creates, individuals can use it in their own national courts, just as if it came from a statute passed by their own national parliament. This means treaty provisions have direct effect. There are two types of direct effect: vertical direct effect, where individuals are given rights against governments, and horizontal direct effect, where individuals are given rights against other people and organisations. Treaty provisions and regulations have both vertical and horizontal direct effect.

In *Macarthys Ltd* v *Smith* (1980) Mrs Smith was entitled to receive the same pay as her male predecessor in the same job. The UK equal pay legislation, in force before the UK joined the EEC, did not give her that right but she was able to show that Article 141 of the Treaty of Rome gave her this right. She was able to enforce her claim against the company. This case shows how horizontal effect works.

Directives, although not directly applicable, do have vertical direct effect but not horizontal direct effect because they impose obligations on states, not individuals. This direct effect was established in *Van Duyn* v *Home Office* (1974). The Home Office ban on Van Duyn, entering the UK due to belonging to a religious group which the government wanted to exclude, breached the right of freedom of movement within the community.

If there is failure to implement a directive or it has been implemented defectively, but the directive is clear and gives individual rights, it still has vertical direct effect. The fact that directives do not have horizontal direct effect was stated in *Duke* v *GEC Reliance Ltd* (1988). Mrs Duke's employer was a private company so she was unable to rely on the Equal Treatment Directive. Perhaps because of the unfairness of this, the concept of the state has been quite widely drawn and has been held to cover the Health Authority in *Marshall* v *Southampton and South West Hampshire Area Health Authority* (1986). The Health Authority was held to be 'an arm of the state' and as the directive had vertical direct effect, Mrs Marshall could rely on it.

🖉 The differences between vertical direct effect and horizontal direct effect are recognised. The areas in which direct effect applies are illustrated with appropriate, well-developed cases.

It can be seen that membership of the EU has had a great effect on the supremacy of Parliament. As a result there are certain areas where Parliament has to accept the laws from the EU instead of being able to make its own. However, in other areas of law Parliament is still the supreme law maker, being able to legislate as it sees fit. It should also be said that s.2 of the European Communities Act can theoretically be amended or repealed, but this is highly unlikely while the UK remains in the EU. If the UK does decide to leave the EU, s.2 can be revoked and Parliamentary supremacy would be regained.

🖉 The answer concludes with reference to the way in which Parliamentary supremacy may be regained. This part of the question could be answered by looking at a number of other relevant factors. The examiner is usually looking for sound understanding of two of the relevant issues. Here the effects on the supremacy of Parliament and the ways in which the laws take effect have been selected. The candidate has demonstrated sound knowledge supported by appropriate examples. The answer would be worth **18 out of 20 marks**.

■ ■ ■

C-grade answer

(a) The sources of European law are treaties, regulations, directives and decisions. Treaties set out the main aims of the EU. They are the most important source of law.

The EU makes regulations, directives and decisions, under Article 249 of the Treaty of Rome, which are the types of European law. Regulations are binding on all member states and do not need any law to bring them into effect. This was shown in the Tachograph case.

Directives are directed at member states to make them bring their laws in line with the rest of the Community. There must be some sort of legislation made in the member country to bring them into effect. They cover such areas as equal pay and equal opportunities.

Decisions are aimed at individual companies or states and are only binding on the recipient.

🖉 This candidate shows some understanding of all the sources of law. The source of the power to make some of the types of law is recognised and directives are outlined with some indication of the areas they cover. However, because there is no real explanation or examples in support, this candidate would not be awarded more than 5 marks.

(b) One way in which English law has been affected is the way in which the courts apply the law. EU law has to take priority over the country's own laws. The courts will not apply the law if it conflicts with EU law. This happened in the *Factortame* case when the Spanish fishermen went to court about the Act which tried to stop them from getting fishing quotas in the UK.

If the English courts are not sure if the UK law is the same as the EU law, they can make a reference to the European Court of Justice. This is called an Article 234 reference. They can ask the ECJ if the UK law is right. This happened in *Macarthys* v *Smith* where the laws on equal pay were not in line with the Treaty of Rome, which said that men and women should be paid the same for doing the same jobs.

Once the ECJ has made a ruling on a matter, all the courts must follow it. This means that when judges are following precedent, if the case involves EU law they must follow any precedent set by the ECJ. In addition, when carrying out statutory interpretation, particularly in areas of EU law, the judges must look at the purpose of the legislation, taking a purposive approach rather than one of the three 'rules'. This is because treaty provisions only set principles, not necessarily how they should be carried out.

Membership of the EU has brought about many changes in the law in the UK. It has introduced the use of tachographs in lorries so that drivers do not spend too long driving. The Equal Opportunities Directives have resulted in men being entitled to free prescriptions and bus passes when they reach 60 instead of 65, bringing them into line with women.

This candidate has taken a different but equally creditworthy approach to this part of the question. All the areas covered are relevant but the answer lacks depth. A fuller explanation of the Preliminary Rulings Procedure and the situations in which it should be used would have gained more marks. This answer would be worth 11 marks.

Statute law

Describe and evaluate the formal process used in creating a statute.　　(20 marks)

e This topic is usually examined as part of a question, the other part being concerned with other aspects such as influences on Parliament.

■ ■ ■

A-grade answer

The formal process of creating a statute involves both Houses of Parliament — the House of Commons and the House of Lords. All statutes start life as a bill. This may be in the form of a public bill or a private bill. Public bills, the most common, are usually introduced by the government, but some are private member's bills which are introduced by backbench MPs. The bills introduced by the government have general effect and are concerned with public policy which affects the law of the country. Private bills are usually concerned with local matters and are promoted by such bodies as local authorities or statutory bodies seeking special powers.

e This introduction clearly explains the different types of bill.

All public bills have to undergo a formal procedure in both Houses, which can start in either House. At the first reading, which is purely formal, the title of the bill is read out. At the second reading stage the bill is proposed by the government minister responsible and the House holds a full debate on the general principles of the bill. A vote to see if the bill should go further is taken at the end of the debate. The bill then passes to the committee stage where the committee, consisting of MPs from all the political parties, examines every clause in detail. Amendments can be made at this stage. Once this is completed the committee reports back to the whole House — the report stage. Further amendments may be proposed and voted on. A third reading then takes place when the bill in its final form is presented to the House and the final vote is taken. If the vote is in favour of the bill, it passes to the other House — the House of Lords if it started in the House of Commons — and the same stages are repeated there. In the House of Lords the whole House acts as a committee and all the amendments are debated and voted on. If the House of Lords makes amendments to a bill which started in the Commons, it is referred back to the House of Commons to consider the amendments. Once a bill has successfully passed through all the stages in both Houses it receives the Royal Assent, after which it can become law. This Royal Assent is no longer given in person and the last time it was refused was in 1707. Without Royal Assent the bill could not become law. At this point the bill becomes an Act of Parliament.

e The candidate shows sound knowledge of the roles played by both Houses of Parliament and the Crown in the creation of an Act of Parliament. The difference in the procedure at the committee stage in the House of Lords is also noted.

The MPs in the House of Commons are democratically elected and, as such, they are legitimately entitled to take part in the legislative process. However, there is some criticism over the fact that the House of Lords is involved. The members of the House of Lords are not elected and this is seen as undemocratic, especially if they can prevent government sponsored bills from being passed. At one time they could do this but the Parliament Acts of 1911 and 1949 have changed this. If the House of Lords rejects a bill, provided it passes through all the necessary stages in the House of Commons in the next parliamentary session, it can become law. The House of Lords is considered to be a check on the executive's powers, acting as a safeguard to the abuse of power. It has made the government rethink its proposals at times, such as the plans to abolish jury trial for some offences.

> 🖉 There is sound recognition of the role of the House of Lords as a check on the government and the restrictions on the government's powers.

The process of statute creation can be a slow, cumbersome procedure but it does allow important bills which deal with major issues of economic and social policy to receive adequate debate and scrutiny before they become law. However, it is possible to pass emergency legislation quickly if necessary, as with the Football (Disorder) Act 2000. Even if there are doubts about the efficiency of the proposals, a government with a secure majority can have its proposals enacted without significant amendments, as happened with the Dangerous Dogs Act 1991. However, the formal process for each bill must be completed in the parliamentary session in which it was started or it will not become law. This often means that the time to debate all the issues will be curtailed and perhaps problems with the legislation missed.

The number of changes which can be made to the original bill may also lead to similar problems so that the final provisions in the Act might not be as originally intended. This may only come to light when a case comes before a judge for statutory interpretation. This may result in the original Act having to be amended, as was the case with the Restriction of Offensive Weapons Act 1959, after the decision in *Fisher* v *Bell* that knives in a shop window were not an offer to sell.

Despite the problems which might occur with some Acts of Parliament, the process is still the most democratic way in which to enact legislation as it gives the elected members of Parliament the chance to put forward their views and to achieve legislation which is acceptable.

> 🖉 This question requires an answer involving the presentation of factual material explaining the legislative process and also evaluation of the process by considering such issues as democracy, speed and quality of legislation. The answer has been developed systematically, setting out the process of statute formation and then discussing each issue in turn. It is important to include some examples to support the evaluation required by the question. Candidates who wrote a very good description of the process in Parliament but failed to introduce any evaluation would do themselves a disservice; no matter how sound the description, they would be unable to achieve more than 11 marks. This shows how important it is to answer the question properly. This answer would be awarded 16 marks.

question

C-grade answer

Parliament — the House of Commons and the House of Lords — is involved in creating statutes (Acts of Parliament). Acts of Parliament start life as bills which set out the proposed legislation. There are two types of bill: public, introduced by the government, and private, introduced on the behalf of public bodies. All bills must pass through all the stages in Parliament before they become law. The process can start in either House but the procedures are the same. At the first reading the bill is introduced to the House of Commons. The second reading takes place when the bill is debated fully and a vote is taken to see if the bill should proceed any further. If the vote is 'yes', the bill goes to the committee stage where a committee of MPs from all the parties examines the bill in detail. Amendments can be made at this stage. The committee reports back to the House — this is the report stage. Further amendments can be made and voted on. The third reading takes place when the bill, in its final form, is voted on. If the bill is passed, it then moves to the House of Lords where the same procedure takes place. There is one difference in that the whole of the House of Lords forms the committee at that stage. If any amendments are made, the bill has to go back to the House of Commons for them to be approved. Once the bill has been passed by both Houses it cannot become law until it has been given the Royal Assent by the Queen. This is a pure formality.

> 🖉 The candidate has briefly described the process in the House of Commons and the House of Lords and referred to the role of the Crown.

In a democracy only those elected to government should be involved in law making. The MPs in the House of Commons are elected by the people in the UK but the members of the House of Lords are unelected. This can be considered as undemocratic, but the House of Lords has an important role to play as it acts as a check on the government. The House can make the government think again about its proposals for the law by making changes to the bill. At one time the House of Lords could prevent a bill from being passed, but that is not possible now.

The process of passing an Act of Parliament can take months, especially if it is a controversial bill. This means that it is a very slow way of changing the law, although sometimes it is possible to pass an Act very quickly. However, this may result in problems in interpretation when the law is enforced, because the details have not been looked at carefully. If the law is found not to work as planned, it then takes time to change it.

Another problem is that if a large number of amendments have been made at the committee stage, the bill may be very different from that which was originally put forward. This is because different MPs will all have different ideas as to what the law should be in that area.

> 🖉 There is some evaluation of the processes involved, particularly the issues concerning the House of Lords, but there is a lack of examples to illustrate any of the issues raised. This is important as the lack of examples may result in a candidate being unable to achieve more than a limited number of marks, no matter how good the rest of the answer is. This answer would be worth 11 marks.

Question 3

Delegated legislation

(a) Describe the different types of delegated legislation, explaining how the power to make them is delegated. *(15 marks)*

(b) Describe how delegated legislation is controlled by both the courts and Parliament. Consider the effectiveness of these controls. *(15 marks)*

■ ■ ■

A-grade answer

(a) Delegated legislation (secondary legislation) is legislation which is not made by Parliament but with its authority. Many of the Acts which are passed by Parliament lay out a basic framework instead of setting out the detailed way in which the law should work. The power to create the detailed rules is delegated to government departments, local authorities or public bodies. This type of statute is called an enabling Act. Examples of this type of Act are the Health and Safety at Work Act 1974 and the Court and Legal Services Act 1990. Unlike Parliament, which has unlimited powers, the delegated powers are limited and are defined in the enabling Act. The European Communities Act 1972 delegates power to enable Community law to be given effect.

Delegated legislation can take one of three forms depending on the body which is authorised to make it. Orders in Council are made by the Privy Council. They are used when it would be inappropriate to use a statutory instrument, such as when transferring responsibilities between government departments. These were used to transfer powers from ministers in the UK government to the ministers in the devolved assembly in Scotland. If Parliament is not sitting and there is an emergency, the Queen and Privy Council may make an Order in Council, as in the fuel crisis in 2000. This power is found in the Emergency Powers Act 1920.

Ministers and government departments can be given the power in the enabling Act to make statutory instruments relating to the jurisdiction of their ministry. These take the form of rules, regulations and orders. They apply to the whole country in their effect. They cover such areas as road traffic signs and town and country planning general development orders. Directives from the EU are also implemented in the form of statutory instruments, for example the Unfair Terms in Consumer Contract Regulations. The Lord Chancellor has the power to make delegated legislation under the Access to Justice Act 1999.

The last form of delegated legislation is bylaws. These are made by local authorities such as county or district councils. They are local in ~ff applying in the area of the council concerned, and are involved wit. as parking restrictions, activities which can or cannot be carried c public places. Some public bodies such as British Rail can make bylav rules covering behaviour in public places, for example the ban on smc London Underground.

This answer shows clear understanding of the different types of delegated legislation, which is supported by relevant examples of each type, and the bodies empowered to make them. The purpose of the enabling Act is explained and examples given. All areas required are well covered. This response would be worth 13 marks.

(b) Delegated legislation is controlled by Parliament and the courts. This is to ensure that the delegated powers are not abused.

Parliament has limited control at the time the enabling Act is made as it sets out the extent of the delegated powers in the Act. The Delegated Powers Scrutiny Committee in the House of Lords also looks at all legislation which delegates powers to see if the powers which are delegated are inappropriate. All delegated legislation has to be laid before Parliament before it can come into force. Delegated legislation is subject to either an affirmative resolution, where both Houses of Parliament have to vote, approving the legislation within a certain time period, or a negative resolution, where the legislation is laid before Parliament and if no member puts down a motion to annul it, within a specified period (40 days), it becomes law.

The Joint Committee on Statutory Instruments, the Scrutiny Committee, composed of members from both Houses of Parliament, reviews all statutory instruments. It can draw Parliament's attention to those that need special consideration. If a statutory instrument imposes a tax, is defective, needs clarification or exceeds the powers granted in the Act, it will be referred back to Parliament. Parliament itself holds the ultimate safeguard because it can withdraw the delegated powers and revoke a piece of delegated legislation at any time.

 All aspects of the controls that Parliament has over delegated legislation are well covered.

Delegated legislation can be challenged in the courts. Any person who has a personal interest in the delegated legislation (is affected by it) may apply to the court under the judicial review procedure. This is on the grounds that the delegated legislation is *ultra vires*, i.e. it goes beyond the powers granted by Parliament. This can either be in the form of procedural *ultra vires* where a public authority has not followed the proper procedure set out in the enabling Act, as in *Agricultural, Horticultural and Forestry Training Board* v *Aylesbury Mushrooms Ltd*, where the Ministry failed to consult the interested parties; or substantive *ultra vires*, where the delegated legislation exceeds the powers in the enabling Act, as in *R* v *Home Secretary, ex parte Fire Brigades Union*. The changes the Home Secretary made to the Criminal Injuries Compensation Scheme exceeded his powers in the Criminal Justice Act 1988.

 The grounds for judicial review are explained well, with both procedural and substantive *ultra vires* being explained. Relevant cases are given in support.

The controls by Parliament have drawbacks. One major problem is the fact that there are over 3,000 statutory instruments made each year. This has the effect that some pieces of legislation which may not be suitable may slip through the review procedure. The affirmative procedure does draw Parliament's attention to the delegated legislation, but it is only possible on rare occasions to prevent the legislation from being passed. The committee in the House of Lords has limited powers. Although it reports to the House of Lords before the committee stage, it has no power to amend the bill. The Scrutiny Committee is more important and has had some success in having changes made to some pieces of delegated legislation. It lacks power because it can only consider whether the delegated powers have been used properly and not the merits of the legislation. Its reports are not binding.

Control by the courts has been more successful, with many challenges being upheld, but even this has problems. It relies on individuals who are affected by the legislation bringing a case to court. This can be a costly and time-consuming business. The delegated legislation may have been in force for years before it is challenged. In addition, the discretionary powers conferred on the minister under the Act may be extremely wide, making it difficult to establish that he has acted *ultra vires*.

Despite these problems, it is important to have controls over delegated legislation, and they have been shown to work in some instances, which is better than having no controls at all. However, as said before, Parliament does have the power to repeal the enabling Act, which is an important safeguard.

This part of the question requires factual explanation of the ways delegated legislation is controlled, followed by evaluation of these. This is carried out in a systematic way, with a final conclusive paragraph. It is important that some evaluation is attempted when required by a question. Failure to do so, no matter how well presented the factual element is, will result in a lower mark. As this question addresses the relevant issues it would be worth 14 marks.

■ ■ ■

E-grade answer

(a) Parliament is too busy to maintain and make new legislation, as many issues need resolving at any one time and Parliament members are not experts in all fields of law. It has become necessary for Parliament to delegate the power to make new legislation to other bodies. The main delegation is in three areas:

(i) Orders in Council — used mainly in emergency situations when Parliament is not sitting. These legislative processes are made by the monarch and the Privy Council and are rarely used.

(ii) Statutory instruments — government ministers are responsible for their own areas of work. Legislation is written, then Parliament approached to accept or dismiss the new Act. So, it can be seen that ministers regulate this legislation.

(iii) Bylaws — legislation made on local issues by local councils, for example parking problems.

The candidate states that Parliament can delegate powers to make delegated legislation but gives no explanation of how this done. The different types of delegated legislation are named and an example of bylaws given. The material in the answer shows some understanding but the discussion is superficial. Statutory Instruments should not be referred to as Acts. The mark for this question includes credit for material included in (b) and it would be awarded 7 out of 15 marks.

(b) Delegated legislation is controlled by both Parliament and the courts. Parliament controls it by ministers being responsible for their own areas, for example the Lord Chancellor is able to control and make legislation on Access to Justice. The health minister is responsible for health and safety legislation. Each expert has his own field of responsibility.

This information is relevant to part (a). The examiner is allowed to give credit for this, which is reflected in the mark for (a), but this is not as high a mark as when the material is written in the correct section. It is permissible to refer back to material in an earlier part of the question if it is relevant and you wish to save time.

When a new legislation is proposed, Parliament discusses the issues and gives either an affirmative or dismissive answer. The problem may occur when legislation is passed and used prior to Parliament discussing it, as the legislation is effective from the date when it is written, not when it is discussed by Parliament. Consequently, negative legislation can be in force prior to it being dismissed.

The higher courts have the power to overrule delegated legislation if it is thought that the legislation was written over and above the power of the person writing it. The power is over and above the minister's responsibility. Therefore, the courts have the power over ministers and if legislation can be overruled, are the right people making it? Is it consistent and reliable?

It is a difficult issue to address as there are too many areas which need legislation, but experts in each field must be used to ensure its relevance. Delegated legislation may be the only way to ensure speedy decision making in an area which is so vast and needs to change to meet the needs of government and society. At present there appears to be no alternative. It is important that legislation remains relevant and constant to maintain confidence in the system.

The candidate starts off by mentioning the affirmative and negative resolution procedure, although there is some confusion. Again, there is recognition of the role of the courts and the grounds for finding legislation valid. Neither of the controls is developed in any way, and the rest of the material presented is irrelevant to the question. This response has been included in order to show the importance of planning your answer to make sure that the relevant material is included in the right part of the answer. It also shows the importance of learning the material properly. The mark for this part of the question would be worth 5 out of 15 marks. The total mark would make this a borderline E/fail.

Influences on Parliament

(a) **Both before and during the legislative process, Parliament is subject to many influences. Using illustrations, describe these influences.** (20 marks)

(b) **Select two of these influences. Discuss their advantages and disadvantages.** (10 marks)

■ ■ ■

A-grade answer

(a) The influences on Parliament include political considerations such as the party manifesto, law reform agencies and other pressure/interest groups. Parliament itself may seek opinions on changes in the law from bodies which it has set up for this purpose.

The Law Commission was set up in 1965 to advise the government. It is a permanent, full-time body with five Law Commissioners assisted by legally trained staff. The Commission's work involves keeping all areas of law under review and producing a systematic programme of reform. The Lord Chancellor and other government departments may refer topics to the Law Commission, or it may consider a topic of its choice after gaining government approval.

The Commission researches an area of law and then produces a consultative paper setting out the present law, the problems with it and any proposals for change. Interested parties are able to put forward their views and a final report is published. This sets out any recommendations, and a draft bill if legislation is proposed. The bill will only become law if Parliament decides to proceed with it and it undergoes the parliamentary process to become an Act of Parliament. Legislation which has resulted from this process includes the Law Reform (Year and a Day Rule) Act 1996 and the Contract (Rights of Third Parties) Act 1999. There have been over 100 proposals put forward and about 70% have been adopted.

Temporary committees may also be set up by Parliament to review a certain area of law. These are called Royal Commissions and once their work is complete and their report is made, they are disbanded. They can have research carried out on their behalf and interested parties can give their views. Important changes in the law have resulted from Royal Commissions. The Royal Commission on Criminal Justice 1993, set up after several highly-publicised cases of miscarriage of justice, resulted in the Criminal Appeal Act 1995. The Police and Criminal Evidence Act 1984 was also the result of a Royal Commission report.

> 🖉 The role of these two important law reform advisory agencies is explained using adequate examples of the results of their influence on the legislation passed by Parliament.

A third area of influence is pressure groups. They are independent of Parliament. These are bodies of people with a shared interest in getting the government to change the law in certain areas. Some aim to get their items onto the legislative agenda while others adopt a moral campaign, for example the National Viewers and Listeners Organisation, which was inspired by the late Mary Whitehouse. They may be groups with a cause, such as Shelter, Help the Aged, Friends of the Earth and Greenpeace, or groups with a sectional interest, such as the Confederation of British Industry and trade unions, and cover many different areas of concern. Pressure groups try to achieve their aims by targeting politicians, civil servants and local government offices. They lobby MPs, organise petitions and gain as much publicity for their cause as possible. Some groups are well organised, some are large, and some are small. At times they may join forces, as happened recently when those opposed to the proposed legislation to ban fox hunting held a joint march with the Countryside Alliance. Some pressure groups only exist for a short time as they are set up to deal with a specific issue. Once that issue is resolved they disband. A pressure group may be set up as the result of a tragic incident, such as the killing of the young school children in the Dunblane massacre in 1996. A successful campaign to ban the private ownership of handguns was launched. Even if a pressure group is able to present its arguments, this does not mean that its views will be taken into consideration.

Some pressure groups are more successful than others. Larger groups are likely to be more successful than smaller ones, but sometimes being able to grab the attention of the media and being persistent can pay off. Mary Whitehouse was a persistent campaigner against child pornography and was instrumental in getting the government to introduce the Protection of Children Act 1978. The more power the group has, the more likely it is to be able to influence legislation. Organisations concerned with big business are particularly effective. However, Shelter was successful in persuading the government to introduce change for homeless people in the Housing Homeless Persons Act 1977. The government now has to consider the environmental impact of its policies because of the way in which Greenpeace and the Friends of the Earth have heightened public awareness of environmental issues.

> The second part of this answer shows good knowledge of how pressure groups work and the sorts of areas in which they are involved. The potential content for this question is quite wide as there are several influences that could be considered. The answer to the question could be addressed in two ways. The first would be to describe two of the influences comprehensively with appropriate illustration. The second would be to show sound understanding of three or more influences with less comprehensive explanation and some illustration. This is the approach taken in this answer, where the candidate has selected two influences which have been set up by the government and another where the groups are independent of Parliament. This answer would be awarded **16 marks**.

(b) One of the advantages of the Law Commission is that it has access to Parliament. The government can decide the areas of law which it wants reviewed and therefore those areas are more likely to become legislation, especially if they were proposed by the Lord Chancellor's department. Another advantage is the fact that the Law Commission can research the area thoroughly, and by the consultation process is able to obtain a cross-section of views from people who will be affected by the legislation. The proposed legislation will be well suited for its purpose. The Law Commission is also able to select its own areas to review. Another advantage is the expertise that the legally qualified staff are able to bring to their work.

The disadvantages include the fact that it is not really independent, as the areas it reviews are put forward by the government. Even when it selects its own area for review, it has to have the permission of the government to carry it out. Although the Law Commission is asked by the government to review the law, this does not mean that all its proposals will be accepted. The draft code for Criminal Law was put forward in1985 but has never been acted on.

One of the advantages of pressure groups is that they represent public opinion. They are also independent of Parliament. Pressure groups are able to inform and stimulate public debate. Weaker groups in society can become involved in the legislative process due to the way in which pressure groups bring people together. They inform the legislature of the need for new legislation in certain areas.

Pressure groups also have disadvantages. Some pressure groups, although relatively small, are able to exert considerably more influence than others because they are well organised and well resourced. They may take more of Parliament's time and attention than other groups. There has also been an increase in professional lobbying agencies, which may disturb the democratic process. Even if a pressure group does manage to present its arguments, this does not mean that it will have any influence.

🖉 This answer shows sound understanding of both the advantages and disadvantages of the two influences. It would be worth 8 out of 10 marks.

■ ■ ■

C-grade answer

(a) The influences on Parliament include political pressure, pressure groups, the media and law reform agencies. Before an election each political party sets out its plans in a party manifesto. These are the proposals which it will make law if it forms the government.

Pressure groups consist of people who share a common interest in getting the government to change the law in certain areas. They may represent a cause such as Shelter on homelessness or Friends of the Earth on environmental matters, or interest groups such as the Confederation of British Industry, trade unions or professional organisations such as the Law Society. They target politicians by lobbying MPs, organising petitions and gaining as much publicity for their cause as possible. At times groups may link together to support a common cause. Some pressure groups have many members, but some are only small. Sometimes a pressure group may only come into existence for a limited period of time, until the issue in question is resolved.

✏ So far this candidate has given information on the way in which the influences are exerted but there is no reference to any material to illustrate the ways in which the influences work.

The media — newspapers, television and radio — play a part in influencing Parliament by bringing issues to the attention of the government. This is done by giving an issue plenty of coverage in the newspapers, on TV and radio so that it can be brought to the notice of the public.

The general public can also make its views known by writing to newspapers, MPs and government ministers.

The Law Commission, set up by the government, is able to review areas of law to see what reforms can be made. The government can refer areas to the Law Commission for review or it can choose its own topic, with Parliament's approval. It is able to carry out research and consult interested people. Its final proposals are published and presented to Parliament. If there is a proposal to change legislation, a draft bill is included.

If a major problem in the law causes public concern, then a Royal Commission — a temporary committee — may be set up to investigate that area. It is able to have research carried out and interested parties can make submissions. Its final report is presented to the government, which may or may not decide to act on all or some of the recommendations.

✏ This candidate has continued to present a strong account of the various influences on Parliament, but there are no examples of particular reports, campaigns or pieces of legislation which are a result of these influences. This is another example of a candidate failing to provide any illustration when requested to do so by the question. As a result this answer, no matter how good, could not be given more than 15 marks.

(b) The advantage of media pressure is that it brings matters to the attention of the public and the government. It allows members of the public to make their feelings known to the politicians. The disadvantage of media pressure is that the media can actually whip up public opinion over certain matters instead of reflecting it. It may give the impression that something is far worse than it actually is.

The advantage of pressure groups is that they represent public opinion and allow members of the public to express their views on matters. They are also independent of the government, which is good for democracy. The disadvantage is that they do not always succeed in their lobbying. Even if they are able to put their point to Parliament, this does not mean that Parliament will take any notice.

✏ This answer displays clearer understanding of the advantages and disadvantages of the media than of pressure groups. It would receive no more than 5/10 marks, making a good C-grade answer overall.

Statutory interpretation

(a) Explain the different approaches (rules) which a judge may take when
interpreting a statute. (20 marks)

(b) For any two of these approaches, discuss the advantages and disadvantages. (10 marks)

■ ■ ■

A-grade answer

(a) When required to interpret an Act of Parliament a judge can take several different
approaches. The judge may select the one which he or she considers to be the
most appropriate as there is no set order to be followed.

The literal rule requires the judge to look at the words of the Act and give them
their plain, literal meaning, even if this produces an absurd outcome which may
be contrary to that which Parliament intended. In *Fisher* v *Bell* it was an offence to
offer flick-knives for sale. The defendant had flick-knives on show in his shop
window and argued that they were not an 'offer for sale'. The court, applying the
literal approach, said that they were 'invitations to treat', not offers for sale. The
defendant was not guilty.

> ⮑ It is not sufficient merely to cite names of cases; some relevant facts should be
> given so as to reinforce your answer, as is done here.

The golden rule may be used by judges if the literal rule would produce an absurd
result. Where a word has more than one meaning, the judges may choose the one
which produces the least absurd result. In *R* v *Allen*, if the words of the Act had
been given their literal meaning it would have been impossible to commit the
offence of bigamy because you cannot 'marry' another person while still married
to someone else. The court said 'shall marry' meant 'go through a marriage
ceremony' which meant the defendant was guilty.

The mischief rule allows the judge to look at what 'mischief' Parliament was trying
to prevent when it passed the Act. In a case involving the Abortion Act, only 'certified general practitioners' were allowed to carry out abortions. Due to new techniques,
part of the process could be carried out by nurses. The question was, would this be
breaking the law? The court decided that Parliament intended to stop backstreet
abortions and to make sure that abortions were carried out safely. The court interpreted the words to mean 'under the supervision of a certified general practitioner'.

> ⮑ If you cannot remember a case name but do know the facts, these can still be used
> to illustrate your answer as this candidate has done to explain the mischief rule.

The approach which is commonly used today is the purposive approach. This looks
at what Parliament intended the Act to achieve. To find this the judges can use
both intrinsic (internal) aids and extrinsic (external) aids.

☑ There is sound understanding of the three 'rules' used in statutory interpretation which is supported by the use of appropriate cases. The purposive approach is not so well explained.

Intrinsic aids are found in the Act itself. They include the long and short title of the Act, the preamble, if present, setting out Parliament's reasons for the statute, definition sections for words in the Act, schedules and headings for any section or group of sections.

Extrinsic aids are external aids which include dictionaries of the time the Act was made, law reform reports and previous case law. Since *Pepper* v *Hart* (1993), reference to Hansard, the daily report of proceedings in Parliament, is allowed if the legislation is ambiguous or obscure and the matters in question are statements made by a minister introducing the Act and clarify the point at issue. The courts may also refer to international conventions. In *Fothergill* v *Monarch Airlines Ltd* the House of Lords said that preparatory notes published with an international convention could be used. All new bills since 1998 have explanatory notes which explain the background of the bill and can be used by the courts.

☑ Instead of merely stating that the courts can use Hansard, the candidate explains the limitations of its use. The use of intrinsic and extrinsic aids is understood. To reach the top mark band there must be a sound understanding of both the rules of interpretation and the use of the aids, with the use of appropriate cases. Some imbalance is allowed. No reference is made to presumptions or rules of language. This does not matter, but would have been credited if used. This candidate would reach the top mark band and be awarded **18** or **19** marks.

(b) The literal rule has the advantage of maintaining Parliamentary supremacy. Judges, by giving words their literal meaning, are not involved in making law. Another advantage is that a person reading the Act will know what the court's decision on the law will be.

One disadvantage of the literal rule is that it may result in an absurd outcome. This was the case in *Fisher* v *Bell*, where the legislation was clearly aimed at this type of situation. As a result of this decision, Parliament had to amend the Act. The use of the literal rule can also result in unfair/harsh decisions as in *LNER* v *Berriman*, where Mrs Berriman's claim for compensation for the death of her husband, who was killed while oiling points on the railway line, failed because the court held that oiling the points did not come under relaying and repairing the line, for which a lookout had to be provided.

The main advantage of the purposive approach is that judges have the discretion to interpret the Act in such a way as to achieve the purpose that was intended. This type of approach was used in *Smith* v *Hughes*, so that prostitutes soliciting from the windows in a street fell within the relevant Act, which was to allow people to walk down the street without being solicited. This approach removes the necessity for Parliament having to keep amending the law.

The disadvantage of the purposive approach is that when judges use it to interpret an Act so as to get the desired effect, it is argued that they are making law. This goes against the idea of the separation of powers. Judges should not make law; it should be made by the elected members of Parliament.

e This answer focuses on the advantages and disadvantages of the literal and purposive approaches. Again, appropriate cases are used as illustration. A sound understanding would place this response in the top mark band with 9 or 10 marks.

■ ■ ■

C-grade answer

(a) Judges use various approaches to interpret an Act of Parliament to assess what Parliament meant or wanted to avoid being repeated when the Act was made. There are three main rules which judges use. They are not used in any particular order but the literal rule is often used first.

e This candidate makes a good start by recognising that there is no definite order in which judges have to use the 'rules'.

The literal rule attempts to examine what Parliament said when the Act was passed. A case for this is *Fisher* v *Bell*. A shopkeeper had a knife in his shop window but it was not on sale. Under an Act knives were not to be offered for sale. The case argued that by having the knife visible it was on offer, whereas in fact it was to tempt customers into the shop. As the knife was only on display it was not for sale, so it did not contravene the Act.

The golden rule attempts to examine what is meant when deciding the Act. In *R* v *Allen* Parliament said that it was an offence for a person to go through more than one marriage ceremony during their life. If they did, then it was bigamy. What Parliament meant was that a person can only go through one ceremony while being married. If the marriage is annulled by death or divorce or other means, then the person may marry again.

e There is no clear understanding of the literal rule. The golden rule is poorly explained but an appropriate case is cited which helps to compensate.

The mischief rule examines what Act Parliament was trying to prevent when making the law. In *Smith* v *Hughes* the Act stated that prostitution in the streets was illegal. This was about a prostitute sitting in the window of a house. She was soliciting but not in the street, and therefore it was argued that the offence had not taken place. When making the Act Parliament wanted to prevent prostitution. She was found guilty.

Another approach to interpreting an Act of Parliament is the purposive approach which examines what Parliament meant when writing the Act. This looks at methods to support the purpose of the Act, as was seen in *Pepper* v *Hart*. In this case it was debated whether Hansard, which is a record made at the time the Act was discussed in Parliament, could be used to assist the judge in his interpretation. It can explain examples of what Parliament was trying to prevent when making the Act.

question

📝 The explanation of the mischief rule shows good understanding and is developed by using an appropriate case in support. Reference is made to the purposive approach but this would need to be developed further for a higher mark.

Judges can also use intrinsic and extrinsic aids to help interpret an Act.

Intrinsic aids consist of written details attached to the Act, e.g. the long and short titles of the Act, a preamble, written at the beginning of the Act, to aid interpretation and explain the purpose of the Act and any explanatory notes which may be written to support the Act and assist the judge. Explanatory notes are recent and are only just beginning to be used in court as newer Acts are being made.

Extrinsic aids consist of aids outside the Act to assist interpretation, e.g. Hansard, notes written at the time the Act was discussed in Parliament, dictionaries used at the time the Act was made and language used at the time. These two aids are very important in old Acts where wording was used differently from today. Law reports may also be used to aid interpretation.

📝 Intrinsic and extrinsic aids are discussed. However, explanatory notes have wrongly been described as intrinsic aids. The limitations on the use of Hansard have also been left out. As the candidate has demonstrated some understanding of the material required and used some appropriate cases, the answer would be awarded 12 marks.

(b) The advantage of the literal rule is that it attempts to identify what Parliament said when the Act was made. This helps to maintain consistency within the law. By using the literal rule, solicitors and barristers can advise their client of the potential outcome. The disadvantage of the literal rule is that the words used in the Act may be outdated and have a different meaning today than when the Act was issued. This causes inconsistency and unreliability, thus reducing society's confidence in the judiciary.

The advantage of the golden rule is that the reasons behind the Act can be maintained up to date by the judge identifying what Parliament set out to prevent happening. The disadvantage of the golden rule is that different judges interpret instructions and rules differently. Depending upon social and political backgrounds, a judge may interpret an Act to suit the situation.

📝 Both the advantages and disadvantages of two of the 'rules' have been discussed. The comments, however, are brief and unsupported by cases. This response would receive no more than 5 marks. You should be aware that this is only one way in which this topic can be examined. The question could require explanation of the approaches as above, with the second part being an evaluation of the uses of aids. In this case, the marks are likely to be split evenly between both parts, that is 15 marks each. Alternatively, the use of the 'rules' may be asked as part of a question linked to the creation of statutes.

Judicial precedent

(a) Explain and illustrate the operation of the doctrine of judicial precedent. (15 marks)

(b) Using appropriate cases, consider the extent to which judges are bound by their own previous decisions. (15 marks)

■ ■ ■

A-grade answer

(a) When the facts in a case are the same as those in a previous decided case, the doctrine of judicial precedent requires judges to follow those decisions. This is known as *stare decisis* (let the decision stand). The judge's written decision sets out the facts and the legal principles used to reach the decision. The legal principles are known as the *ratio decidendi* (the reason for deciding) and form the binding precedent to be followed in later cases. The neighbour principle in the tort of negligence is from the *ratio decidendi* in *Donoghue v Stevenson*. The reason for this is to provide certainty and consistency in the law. It allows lawyers to look at the facts of a case and if there is already a decision on those facts, they can advise their clients of the likely outcome of any court action.

Not all of the legal principles form the binding precedent. Sometimes a judge will state what he thinks the law would be if the facts were slightly different. This is known as *obiter dicta* and can form persuasive precedent. *Promissory estoppel* was the result of an *obiter dicta* statement by Lord Denning in the *High Trees* case. Persuasive precedent may also result from dissenting judgments, when a case is decided by a majority of judges or from decisions from the Privy Council, as happened from the *Wagon Mound* case — the principle of remoteness of damage in tort.

📝 *Stare decisis, ratio decidendi* and *obiter dicta* are explained and appropriate examples given.

To make sure that the doctrine works, a court hierarchy has developed whereby in the English court system the lower courts are bound by the decisions of those above them. If the case concerns EU law, then the courts are all bound to follow previous judgments of the European Court of Justice. Otherwise the highest court is the House of Lords (HL). All the other courts in England have to follow the decisions of the HL. The case of *London Street Tramways* v *London County Council* (1898) established the fact that the HL was bound by its own previous decisions, but the Practice Statement made by the HL in 1966 allows it to depart from its own previous decisions when it appears right to do so.

The court below the HL is the Court of Appeal (CA), which is bound to follow the decisions of the HL. The CA consists of two divisions, the Civil Division and the Criminal Division. The Civil Division is also bound to follow its own previous decisions, but in *Young* v *Bristol Aeroplane Co Ltd* (1944) three exceptions were listed.

These are:
- where a previous decision was made *per incuriam* (in error)
- where there are two conflicting decisions
- where a later decision of the HL overrules a previous decision in the CA

The Criminal Division is bound by its own previous decisions, with the exceptions in *Young's* case or if someone's liberty is in issue.

The next court in the hierarchy is the High Court, which is composed of the divisional courts and the ordinary High Court. These courts are bound by the HL and the CA. The Chancery and Family Divisions are bound by their own previous decisions. These decisions are also binding on the ordinary High Court, but this court is not normally bound by its own decisions.

The crown court, county court and magistrates' court are all bound by the decisions of all the courts above them. They are not bound by their own previous decisions.

With so many cases being heard every year, there has to be some way in which the lawyers/judges can find out which decisions they must follow. To make sure that this is achieved, a comprehensive system of law reporting has been established. The judgment, in every case that is decided in the courts which set the precedents, is written down and published in these reports, for example the *All England Law Reports*, the *Weekly Law Reports*.

> An adequate, accurate explanation of the hierarchy of the courts is essential when answering a question on how precedent works. The position in the HL and the CA is very important, but the position of the lower courts should also be covered. No question on this topic can be answered properly if *ratio decidendi* is not covered. It is not sufficient merely to identify and define it. There must be some explanation with case material in support. As precedent is based on decided cases, the use of cases is essential in the answer. Merely citing the case name is not enough; the principles of the case should be given. Another important feature that is often overlooked is the necessity for a system of law reporting. This answer would earn 13 marks.

(b) As already stated in (a), the courts must follow precedent where the facts of a case are the same as a previously decided one, even if the decision was considered to be a bad one or opinions have changed since the case was decided. The ways in which the courts are bound by their own previous decisions and the higher courts have been described above.

> This shows how you can refer back to material which supports your points included in an earlier part of the answer.

However, the courts have several methods by which they can avoid following precedent. The courts may be able to distinguish the case under consideration from that in which the precedent was set. They may decide that there is a difference in the facts of the two cases so there is no need to follow the precedent. The CA used this method in *Boardman* v *Sanderson* (1964), where it was able to depart from the decision in *King* v *Phillips* (1953). In both cases, the parent of a child had heard screams when their child's bicycle was run over by a car. Neither parent saw the accident but each claimed they had suffered nervous shock. The claim failed in the first case as the child was not injured, but succeeded in the second case because the child was injured.

📝 The best way to show how distinguishing works is either to use cases, as here, or to give an example of two situations in which the facts are similar but there is a slight difference which can be used to distinguish one from the other.

The courts may also be able to distinguish cases by saying that the *ratio* was too widely or too narrowly decided. This is possible because it is the judges who are hearing later cases who decide what the *ratio* in an earlier case is. The court might say that the *ratio* in the previous case, which it wishes to avoid following, is very narrow and does not cover the present case. In some cases, as in the HL and CA, where the original case was heard by more than one judge, each judge may give a different reason for reaching the final decision. This may result in several different *ratios* and subsequent judges can select the one which suits them. At times there may not even be a clear *ratio* in the judgment, so a judge can say that there is no *ratio* to follow.

Judges in the higher courts, that is the HL, can overrule the decisions of the lower court, that is the CA, if they decide that the legal principles are wrong. The 1966 Practice Statement in the HL allows the court to depart from previous decisions where it is right to do so. This means that it can avoid following precedent. The HL has only done so on a few occasions. In *Pepper* v *Hart* the HL overruled the decision in *Davis* v *Johnson* that judges could not refer to Hansard when interpreting a statute. In the latter case the decision of the CA, which had said the courts could use Hansard, had already been overruled. In *R* v *R* (1991) the HL departed from its previous decision when it said that a man could rape his wife. As stated in (a), the CA can depart from its own previous decisions if the exceptions in *Young's* case apply.

It can be seen that judges do have considerable scope to avoid following precedent. This allows the law to be flexible and change as and when it needs to. However, judges do have to bear in mind that there must be certainty in the law and so they should not be too flexible. It is interesting that despite having the ability to depart from their own previous decisions, the HL has only done so in a few cases since 1966.

📝 This is another answer where the use of cases is important to illustrate how the methods work. A few are used here, but you should be able to use the cases you have come across during your study of Unit 3 and in wider reading to enhance your answer. The methods of avoiding having to follow precedent are discussed. In order to obtain a good mark, you must cover all of the methods. It is no good just concentrating on one or two areas such as the Practice Statement and overruling.

question

This answer would benefit from a better assessment and perhaps more suitable cases. It would be awarded 12 marks out of 15.

■ ■ ■

C-grade answer

(a) The system of judicial precedent which operates in the English courts is one where the past decisions of judges create law, which judges in later cases must follow (through the established hierarchy of the court system).

The system of precedence is based on the Latin term *stare decisis* — to stand by what has been decided; do not unsettle the established. This principle in theory allows for both certainty and fairness in the law. For a precedent to be followed, a judge must give the legal reasons for his decision in his judgment. These legal reasons are known as the *ratio decidendi* or *ratios*. *Ratios* are the principles of law that judges use to come to their decision. It is the *ratio* which creates the precedent to be followed in future cases.

For judicial precedent to exist there must be an ordering or hierarchy of the courts. There are courts which create binding precedent, which means that courts lower in the hierarchy are bound to follow decisions made by them. They are the House of Lords, Court of Appeal, Divisional and High Courts. The crown courts, county courts and magistrates' courts do not create binding precedent in their decisions.

For judicial precedent to work there also needs to be an effective system of law reporting, which are official reports of the court cases.

🖉 This question specifically asks for some form of illustration as part of the answer. There is none in this instance. There is clear understanding of *ratio decidendi*, but the court hierarchy is dealt with very superficially. The necessity for law reporting is briefly mentioned. Even if there was a comprehensive account of the three areas covered here, without any cases this answer would not gain more than 11 marks. In this instance it would be awarded 10 marks out of 15.

(b) The system of judicial binding precedent does in general bind judges to follow the previous decisions of earlier courts, although judges have at their disposal some methods which allow them not to be bound by previous decisions.

One method is distinguishing. A judge will be able to distinguish when he or she is able to demonstrate that there is a difference in the material facts of the case that he or she is deciding and the decision of the past case that has created the precedent. When this occurs the judge in the later case is not bound to follow the existing precedent. In fact, nearly all cases can be distinguished, as the exact circumstances of each case are different from one another. Another method is called reversing. This occurs usually in an appeal court such as the Court of Appeal. Reversing means that a court overturned the decision of a court lower than itself in the court hierarchy because it came to a different interpretation of the law.

Judges are able to overrule a decision if a court decides that the legal rule in an earlier case is wrong. Overruling will come from a court higher in the hierarchy, on a decision of a lower court. The House of Lords has a Practice Statement which allows it to overrule its past decisions, which it would normally have to follow.

To summarise, to a large extent judges are bound by decisions in previous cases, but they are able to avoid being bound by the use of distinguishing, reversing and overruling, and in the House of Lords by the Practice Statement.

Again, no cases are used to illustrate the points being made. Some of the ways in which judges can avoid following precedent have been selected, but the discussion is little more than superficial. This would only be worth 7 marks out of 15.